Gretchen Kraut Collection

GOLIATH digest

Goliath Verlagsgesellschaft mbH
Eschersheimer Landstraße 353, D 60320 Frankfurt/Main

Distribution US and Canada
Goliath: P. O. BOX 136, New York, NY 10035, USA
Goliath™ is a registered trademark in the United States
and/or other countries.

contact@goliathbooks.com
www.goliathbooks.com

Contents
Inhalt

Indroduction English

Germans are not really famous for their great passions or pleasures. Abroad, people like to watch them falling under the tables at carnival or at the October Fest, drunk and merry. Tacitus seems to have known this side. He tells tales of the ancestors of the Germans, in classical Rome. He found them a hard and wild tribe that loved to roam the wilderness, stark naked. Indestructible even then but not really prepared to enjoy lust and pleasure. For centuries thereafter, there was little more than yodelling beneath the leather pants. Their best-loved object, a tank-like car, still boasts its indestructible quality. Then, nobody believed that the Germans might indeed, have a very intimate relationship with pornography.

What is that supposed to be? German pornography? After the war, porn was happily transferred outdoors, to Scandinavia, generously partaking in the nude bathing cult. Or it was banned to the German Democratic Republic, where allegedly, women were more willing than in the West. Dreaming was allowed, beyond the borders. There was however, still something left of the good old German wanderlust, spiced up with a little sado-masochism. Fantasizing in the style of the romantic fairy tales by the Brothers Grimm – Hansel and Gretel locked up in the witch's house. What did go on in there? Is this typically German? Yes, it is. Only it is hard to see, as the Nazis had turned nude culture, which after all had been Germanic, having been invented in Germany, into erotic machinery. All steel-hard boys and Arian women, always willing to do what they were asked to do. Germany militarised the erotic, which was permitted to remain pornographic abroad. The time had come for Germans, characterized by war-time rape and a greatly reduced male population, to put their past skeletons in the closet.

Indeed, the Germans had lost something very important. This book shows what they lost: the legendary roaring twen-

ties, when after World War I they shook off the senselessness of the Age of the Kaiser like a drunken stupor. It was the time when photography commenced its victory march, and dared all, without shame.

It was not before the revolutionary sixties that lust was raised its head once more. Until then, 8-mm trash films and mags rotted away in farm barns. German pornography found its subjects close to the bestial, close to the stables. Only the sexual revolution and the simultaneous invention of video reopened the floodgates to the rest of the world. Today, everything is united by the dream, of a time in Germany, which not even the Germans seem to understand. It is the global myth, telling us about the first half of the 20th century, when the erotic vaudeville theatres in Munich, Berlin and Hamburg were fucking-full with exciting ladies, for the high society who could afford it. A lot of sexual experimentation was going on then, despite the censoring and the vice police, when the Germans shed uniforms and corsets to take a breath of fresh morning air. Two hundred photos, almost all from one private collection, show you these sparkling days; the high time when pornographic pictures were still sensational and daring, coquettish and provoking, hot but most of all: prohibited.

Have fun!

Vorwort Deutsch

Mit den Deutschen verbindet man nicht unbedingt große Leidenschaften und Freuden. Im Ausland sieht man es zwar gern, wenn sie zu Karneval und zum Oktoberfest in trinkseliger Ausgelassenheit unter die Tische sinken. Das passt auch irgendwie zu Tacitus, der von den Vorfahren der Deutschen im alten Rom berichtete: Es sei ein besonders hartes und wildes Volk, das nackt durch die Wildnis rannte. Unkaputtbar waren sie damals schon, aber das sind wohl eher schlechte Voraussetzungen, um den Deutschen genussvolle Lustbarkeiten zuzutrauen. Wo unter der Lederhose Jahrhunderte später bestenfalls gejodelt wurde und ihr liebstes Objekt, ein panzerartiges Auto, mit immer noch unkaputtbarer Qualität protzte, da glaubt doch keiner, dass ausgerechnet die Deutschen ein besonders intimes Verhältnis zur Pornografie pflegen würden.

Was wäre denn das auch: deutsche Pornografie? Nach dem Krieg wurde sie gern in die Natur verlegt, nach Skandinavien, freizügig ummäntelt vom Nacktbadekult. Oder in die DDR verbannt, weil man den Frauen unterstellte, sie seien williger als Westmädels. Träumen durfte man ja noch. Jenseits der Grenzen. Da steckt noch der gute alte deutsche Wandervogel drin, der gern auch etwas sadomasochistisch im Namen der romantischen Märchen der Gebrüder Grimm denken darf – Hänsel und Gretel eingesperrt im Hexenhaus. Was da wohl abging?

Ist das typisch deutsch? Ja, das ist es. Man sieht es nur nicht so genau, weil die Nazis die Freikörperkultur, die immerhin ganz germanisch in Deutschland erfunden wurde, in eine erotische Maschine umgossen – lauter stählerne Jungs und arisch reine Frauen, allzeit zu allem bereit. Was als Erotik in Deutschland militarisiert wurde, durfte im Ausland ohne jeden Beigeschmack pornografisch bleiben. Für die Deutschen, von Kriegsvergewaltigung und Männermangel geprägt, war die Zeit dagegen reif, um ihre Vergangenheit in den Giftschrank zu stecken.

Tatsächlich hatten die Deutschen etwas sehr Wichtiges verloren, und dieses Buch zeigt es Ihnen: jene legendären Goldenen Zwanziger Jahre, als nach dem 1. Weltkrieg die Sinnlosigkeit der Kaiserzeit wie in einem Rausch von den Deutschen abfiel. Damals, als die Fotografie ihren Siegeszug antrat, um – auch – schamlos sein zu dürfen. Die Inszenierung der Lust, sie wurde in Deutschland erst in den revolutionären 1960ern wieder aufgenommen. Bis dahin vegetierten 8-mm-Filmchen und Heftchen in Bauernscheunen; deutsche Pornografie fand ihr Metier nah am Vieh, im Stall. Es war die sexuelle Revolution und die zeitgleiche Erfindung des Videos, die endlich die Schleusen zur restlichen Welt wieder öffneten. Was heute alle eint, ist der Traum von einer Zeit in Deutschland, die selbst die Deutschen heute kaum begreifen. Es ist der globale Mythos, der von der ersten Hälfte des 20. Jahrhunderts erzählt, als das erotische Varieté in München, Berlin und Hamburg bumsvoll war mit aufregenden Damen für eine zahlungskräftige Haute Volée. Als sexuell ordentlich experimentiert wurde, gegen die Zensur und die Sittenpolizei, damals, als der Deutsche aus seiner Uniform, als die Deutsche aus ihrem Korsett stieg, um Morgenluft zu wittern. Zweihundert Fotos, fast alle aus einer Privatsammlung, zeigen Ihnen diese Glanzzeit, als pornografische Bilder noch sensationell und dreist, neckisch und provozierend, heiß und – vor allem – verboten waren.

Viel Spaß!

Préambule Français

L'image des Allemands n'est pas nécessairement celle de passions et de plaisirs débordants. Certes à l'étranger on aime les voir s'affaler sous les tables pendant le carnaval et à la fête de la bière à Munich dans une exubérante propension à l'ivresse. Un cliché qui évoque d'une certaine manière les récits de Tacite dans la Rome antique à propos des ancêtres des Allemands : Un peuple particulièrement rude et sauvage courant nu dans les contrées sauvages. Déjà à l'époque, les Allemands étaient invincibles, des dispositions qui n'incitaient certainement pas à leur prêter des penchants pour l'orgie. Bien des siècles plus tard, alors qu'ils iodlent tout au plus dans une culotte de peau et que leur objet favori reste une voiture aussi solide qu'un tank, ce qui leur vaut de toujours se targuer d'une qualité à toute épreuve, personne ne peut encore croire que précisément les Allemands entretiendraient une relation intimiste avec la pornographie.

Qu'est-ce que c'est alors, la pornographie allemande ? Après la guerre, on l'a volontiers expédiée dans la nature, en Scandinavie, enrubannée avec audace du culte de la baignade dans le plus simple appareil. Ou son confinement à la RDA, parce qu'on prêtait aux femmes de l'autre côté d'être plus consentantes que les filles de l'Ouest. Le rêve était encore permis. Au-delà des frontières. Le bon vieux Wandervogel allemand qui s'autorise encore quelque pensée sadomasochiste au nom des contes romantiques des frères Grimm, Hansel et Gretel enfermés dans la maison de la sorcière (où tout est possible), n'est pas tout à fait mort.

Mais est-ce typiquement allemand ? Oui, précisément. On ne s'en aperçoit pas immédiatement parce que les Nazis ont transformé en machine érotique un naturisme du reste inventé en Allemagne dans un esprit tout germanique : rien que des jeunes hommes taillés dans l'acier et des femmes pure race aryenne, prêts à tout et tout le temps. La part d'érotisme qui a in-

tégré le militaire en Allemagne pouvait à l'étranger rester apparenté à de la pure pornographie. Pour les Allemands, marqués par les viols de la guerre et la pénurie d'hommes, l'heure était venue par contre de ranger leur histoire dans l'armoire aux poisons.

Les Allemands avaient effectivement perdu quelque chose de très important et cet ouvrage nous le montre : les années 20, les fameuses années folles, quand au lendemain de la Première Guerre mondiale les Allemands ont, comme dans un état d'ivresse, rompu avec l'absurde époque impériale. A une époque où la photographie allait faire son entrée triomphale pour pouvoir être impudique elle aussi. La mise en scène de la luxure n'allait être reprise en Allemagne que dans les années 60 de la contestation. Jusque là, les petits films 8 mm et les revues avaient attendu dans des granges de ferme ; la pornographie allemande évoluait tout près du bétail dans les étables. La révolution sexuelle et, dans le même temps, l'apparition des vidéos allaient enfin rouvrir les portes vers le reste du monde. Ce qui unit tout ceci aujourd'hui, c'est la nostalgie d'une époque en Allemagne que même les Allemands ont peine à comprendre aujourd'hui. Le mythe universel qui raconte la première moitié du 20ème siècle, du temps où la variété érotique faisait salle comble à Munich, Berlin ou Hambourg avec des femmes exaltantes pour une haute société fortunée. Quand on se livrait à de gentilles expériences sexuelles malgré la censure et la police des mœurs, quand Monsieur enlevait son uniforme et Madame son corset pour flairer l'air du matin. Deux cents photos provenant toutes quasiment d'une collection privée nous montrent cette époque de gloire, du temps où les photos pornographiques étaient encore sensationnelles et osées, coquines et provocantes, torrides mais surtout… interdites.

Bon divertissement

Prologo Español

Los alemanes no damos precisamente una imagen de pasión y alegría. Al pensar en nosotros los extranjeros nos imaginan en el carnaval o en el Oktoberfest, borrachos como cubas. En cierto modo coincide con lo que decía Tácito de nuestros antepasados en la antigua Roma. Se trata de un pueblo rudo y salvaje que corre por los bosques. Ya entonces invencibles, pero sin duda poco propensos a grandes diversiones. Siglos más tarde, cantamos a la tirolesa vestidos con pantalones de cuero, nos pavoneamos en coches descapotables, invencibles. A la vista de las circunstancias, nadie se atreve a pensar que los alemanes mantienen una íntima y especial relación con la pornografía.

¿Qué es exactamente la pornografía alemana? Después de la guerra se trasladó a la naturaleza, a Escandinavia, envuelta en la cultura de la sauna. En la RDA fue prohibida por degradar a la mujer, mostrándola más obediente que las chicas del oeste. Por suerte había espacio para los sueños. Más allá de la frontera. Allí se esconde el viejo explorador alemán, que se divierte pensando en el sadomasoquismo en el nombre de los cuentos románticos de los hermanos Grimm: Hansel y Gretel encerrados en la casa de la bruja. ¿Qué era lo que sucedía en realidad entre las cuatro paredes?

¿Típico de los alemanes? Sí, sin duda. Cuesta verlo, porque los nazis transformaron el culto al cuerpo, que se inventó en Alemania y es una tradición germánica, en una máquina del erotismo: jóvenes musculosos, mujeres arias, puras, listas para todo y en todo momento. Lo que en Alemania se militarizó como erotismo, en el extranjero se tildó de pornografía sin matices. Para los alemanes, marcados por la violencia de la guerra y la falta de hombres, era el momento de olvidar el pasado.

Cierto es que los alemanes habían perdido algo muy importante, y este libro es una muestra de ello: los dorados años

veinte, una época de leyenda. Cuando, después de la primera Guerra Mundial, el sinsentido de la época imperial atrapó con su delirio a los alemanes atreviéndose al descaro. La representación del deseo volvió a retomarse en los revolucionarios años sesenta. Hasta entonces, las películas de superocho y los folletos vegetaban en los graneros de las aldeas. La pornografía alemana se reencontró consigo misma en el ganado, en los establos. La revolución sexual coincidía con la aparición del vídeo, que al fin abría sus puertas al resto del mundo. Lo que hoy en día se ha convertido en el punto de unión es el sueño de una Alemania que a los propios alemanes les cuesta imaginar: es el mito global de los primeros años veinte. La época dorada de los teatros de variedades eróticas de Múnich, Berlín y Hamburgo, de las muchachas de altos vuelos, excitantes y adineradas. Entonces se experimentaba con el sexo de forma metódica, contra la censura y la policía correccional. Entonces los alemanes se quitaban el uniforme, se libraban de sus encorsetadas maneras y disfrutaban del aire fresco de la mañana. Doscientas fotos, casi todas procedentes de una colección privada, le muestran la edad dorada de la fotografía pornográfica: sensacionales, atrevidas, provocadoras, excitantes y, por encima de todo, prohibidas.

Disfrute.

Introduzione Italiano

Che i tedeschi non ci portino a pensare automaticamente a grandi passioni e gioie è un dato di fatto. Lo si può ben notare quando, per carnevale o per l'Oktoberfest, si infilano sotto i tavoli sotto l'effetto di una allegria smodata. Questo valeva in qualche modo anche per Tacito, che riportava degli antenati dei tedeschi nell'antica Roma: "Doveva essere un popolo particolarmente duro e selvaggio, che correva di notte nella natura selvaggia". All'epoca erano già indistruttibili, ma queste sono premesse decisamente negative per poter attribuire ai tedeschi divertimenti pieni di godimento. Là dove, nel migliore dei casi, si faceva jodel con i pantaloni di pelle centinaia di anni dopo, e dove si ostentava il loro oggetto preferito, una macchina tipo panzer dalla qualità sempre indistruttibile, in quanto nessuno ancora crede che proprio i tedeschi culllerebbero un rapporto particolarmente intimo con la pornografia.

Di cosa stiamo parlando quindi: pornografia tedesca? Dopo la guerra è stata rilegata ben volentieri nella natura, in Scandinavia, succintamente avvolta dal culto del bagno notturno. O è stata bandita nella DDR, perchè si attribuiva alle donne di essere più vogliose delle ragazze della Germania occidentale. Qui vi si nasconde ancora il buon vecchio Wandervogel tedesco, che era autorizzato a pensare anche a qualcosa di sadomaso nel nome delle favole romantiche dei fratelli Grimm – Hansel e Gretel – imprigionati nella casa delle streghe. Cosa se ne deduce?

E' tipicamente tedesco? Si lo è. Solo non lo si percepisce così chiaramente, in quanto i nazisti hanno travasato il nudismo, tipicamente tedesco, inventato in Germania, in una macchina erotica – genuini uomini di acciaio e pure donne ariane, sempre pronti a tutto. Quello che è stato militarizzato in Germania come erotismo, poteva rimanere all'estero pornografia senza alcun sapore. Per i tedeschi, plasmati dalla vio-

lenza della guerra e dalla mancanza di uomini, il tempo era al contrario maturo, per nascondere il loro passato nell'armadio dei veleni.

I tedeschi avevano effettivamente perso qualcosa di importante, e questo libro lo mostra loro: quei leggendari dorati anni venti, quando, dopo la prima guerra mondiale, l'insensatezza del periodo del regime calò come cala una sbornia. In quel tempo, quando la fotografia iniziò la sua marcia trionfale, per poter anche essere senza vergogna. La messa in scena del piacere, nuovamente intrapresa in Germania solo nei rivoluzionari anni '60. Fino a quel momento i filmetti 8mm e i giornaletti avevano vegetato nei fienili dei contadini: la pornografia tedesca trovava il suo mestiere vicino al bestiame, nella stalla. Sono stati la rivoluzione sessuale e la contemporanea invenzione del video che hanno aperto finalmente le porte sul resto del mondo. Quello che unisce tutti, oggi, è il sogno di un tempo che fu in Germania, che gli stessi tedeschi oggi a malapena afferrano. E' il mito globale, che racconta della prima metà del ventesimo secolo, quando la varietà erotica a Monaco, Berlino ed Amburgo era piena di "locali" con signore in eccitazione per una Haute Volée a pagamento. E' stato sperimentato come sessualmente regolare, contro la censura e la squadra buoncostume, quando "il tedesco" smetteva la sua uniforme e "la tedesca" il suo corsetto, per fiutare la brezza mattutina. Duecento foto, quasi tutte di una raccolta privata, Vi mostreranno questo splendore, quando le foto pornografiche erano ancora sensazionali e impertinenti, maliziose e provocatorie, bollenti ma soprattutto proibite.

Buon divertimento!

Erotic Postcards

Stephanie Kuhnen

In 1837, French painter and inventor Louis Daguerre succeeded in representing a corner of his studio on a silver plate. An absolutely new medium was born to delight artists as much as peeping toms: photography.

Nudes were among the first Daguerre types. The representation of bodies, directly related to the well-known nudes, in painting and sculpture. The first owners of cameras, then still expensive and rare, were mainly well-off artists. While they began to experiment with design opportunities, many of their students and less well-off peers, used the new technology as a space and cost-saving alternative to live models. These photos soon opened a very new market, with a continuous demand for new illustrations of real persons.

Photographic illustrations representing female nudes attracted many "art lovers." Acquisition "for studies" is a loaded expression, even today and a popular alibi for collectors and consumers of erotic and pornographic photography.

In the late 1850s, several photographers in Germany, Austria and in particular in Berlin and Vienna made their speciality, in-the-nude representations and soon different subjects emerged. While "serious" artists mainly reproduced classical nude poses or classical paintings with professional academic models, other photographers preferred to arrange scenarios parodying folklore or famous paintings, for example oriental harem fantasies which were quite modern at the time. Some started right away with sexually explicit portraits of young women that directly addressed the beholder. Most of their models were prostitutes who loved

this easy way of earning money. Representations of sex, in different variations, were also produced, though illegal. No wonder the photography connoisseur and art lover could find a dealer of this kind of art, in any bordello in the second half of the 19th Century. Most of the bigger brothels offered pornographic photos themselves.

The development of the Wet Plate Collodion process in 1851, for the first time, enabled mass copies from one negative. Readily available to consumers and even more profitable for vendors, these new products created a storm. Many photographers could hardly produce enough photos to satisfy the demand. Police files give a good idea of the total sales volume realized with that kind of photography. The vice squads regularly seized and destroyed large quantities of "obscene illustrations". Erotic and pornographic photography was a profitable, as well as dangerous business, right from the start. Photos were usually made in postcard format and sold in specialized shops such as opticians, art supply stores, select bookstores or street vendors. Of course, they could not exhibit their pictures in public. Therefore a codeword was required to denote the unspeakable, clearly. The term "French Postcard" soon became a synonym of early erotic, photographic and pornographic art.

CABINET-
PHOTOGRAPHIE

+
38.

Die erotische Postkarte

Stephanie Kuhnen

1837 gelang es dem französischen Maler und Erfinder Louis Daguerre, eine Ecke seines Ateliers auf einer Silberplatte abzulichten. Ein völlig neues Medium, das Künstler wie Voyeure gleichermaßen erfreute, war geboren: die Fotografie.

Schon unter den ersten Daguerrotypien befanden sich Akte. Die Körperdarstellungen knüpften direkt an die gängigen Posen von Malerei und Bildhauerei an. Vor allem wohlhabende Künstler gehörten zu den ersten Besitzern der damals noch teuren und seltenen Kameras. Während diese mit den gestalterischen Möglichkeiten zu experimentieren begannen, machten sich viele ihrer Schüler und weniger gut verdienenden Kollegen die platzsparende und kostengünstige Alternative zu lebenden Modellen zu Nutze. Schnell war in diesen Fotografien ein ganz neuer Markt entdeckt, der ständig nach neuen Abbildungen realer Menschen verlangte.

Viele „Kunstfreunde" fanden sich vor allem für die fotografischen Vorlagen, auf denen weibliche Akte abgebildet waren. Der Erwerb zu „Studienzwecken" ist bis heute ein geflügeltes Wort und beliebtes Alibi für Sammler wie Konsumenten erotischer und pornografischer Fotografie.

In den späten 1850ern arbeiteten in Deutschland und Österreich, besonders in Berlin und Wien, mehrere Fotografen spezialisiert mit Aktdarstellungen, wobei sich bereits früh die verschiedenen Sujets herausbildeten. Während die „seriösen" Künstler vor allem antike Nackt-Posen oder klassische Gemälde mit professionellen Akademie-Modellen nachstellten, arrangierten viele Fotografen eher folkloristische und berühmte Gemälde parodierende Szenarien wie die zu der Zeit modernen orientalisch anmuten-

den Haremsfantasien. Einige stellten gleich sexuell explizite, den Betrachter direkt ansprechende Portraits junger Frauen her. Die Modelle fanden sie zumeist unter Prostituierten, die so leicht Geld verdienen konnten. Auch Darstellungen von Sex in den unterschiedlichsten Varianten wurden, wenn auch illegal, produziert. Es verwundert daher nicht, dass der fotografische Kenner und Liebhaber in der zweiten Hälfte des 19. Jahrhunderts in einem Bordell nach einem Händler dieser Art von Kunst fragen konnte. Die meisten größeren Bordelle boten selbst pornografische Fotografien zum Kauf an.

Die Erfindung des nassen Kollodiumverfahrens 1851 ermöglichte erstmals massenweise Abzüge von einem Negativ. Für Konsumenten nun erschwinglich und für Händler noch profitabler, setzte ein Sturm auf diese neuen „Objekte der Begierde" ein. Viele Fotografen kamen mit der Produktion neuer Bilder kaum noch nach. Wie groß der Gesamtumsatz mit solchen Fotografien tatsächlich war, lässt sich teilweise anhand von Polizeiakten rekonstruieren, die regelmäßig große Mengen an „obszönen Darstellungen" beschlagnahmte und vernichtete. Erotische und pornografische Fotografie war von Anfang an ein so einträglich wie gefährliches Geschäft.

Da diese Fotos in gängigen Postkartenformaten angefertigt und in spezialisierten Geschäften wie Optikern, Künstlerbedarfläden, ausgesuchten Buchhandlungen oder eben von Straßenhändlern verkauft wurden, die diese Bilder selbstverständlich nicht öffentlich ausgestellt hielten, bedurfte es eines Codewortes, um das Unbeschreibliche unmissverständlich zu benennen. Die „französische Postkarte" wurde so zum Synonym für frühe fotografische erotische und pornografische Kunst.

541

Through science to justice

Magnus Hirschfeld and the Institute of Sexology

Stephanie Kuhnen

The "Einstein of Sex" was Magnus Hirschfeld, a German Jewish physician, born in 1868. Hirschfeld is also considered the founder of homosexual activism. A homosexual himself, in 1897 in Berlin, together with the publisher Max Spohr, the lawman Eduard Oberg and the writer Max von Bülow, he founded the Scientific Humanitarian Committee (WhK), and was made its President. The committee was the first organisation, worldwide, with the aim of de-criminalizing sexual activities between men. Sexuality between women was not considered a crime under the German emperor Kaiser Wilhelm.

From 1899 until 1923, Hirschfeld published an annual "Yearbook of Intermediate Sexual Stages." Just as Kinsey (the US-American sexologist and biologist) did decades later in the USA, Hirschfeld from 1903, interviewed many students and metal workers on their sexual orientation and evaluated the results in statistics. According to his findings,

the proportion of homosexuals in the German population was 2.3%, and the proportion of bisexuals was 3.4%. At that time, this roused an incredible scandal. Some students sued him for slander. When he was arraigned in court in 1904, the WhK also distanced itself from Hirschfeld and his study, even though or even more so, because it consisted of many gay members.

Hirschfeld's slogan was "Through science to justice." All his life, his main aim was to prove that homosexuality lies in the genes. From the German lawyer and theologist Karl Heinrich Ulrichs (1825 to 1895) he had acquired the theory of a third gender, the human intermediate stage, according to which there were homosexuals, bisexuals, and transsexuals. In that, he differed strongly from the popular theories of the German-Austrian psychiatrist Richard von Krafft-

Ebing (1840 to 1902) and finally also from Sigmund Freud, who both defined homosexuality as a malfunction of the human psyche. The advantage of his interpretation was clear to Hirschfeld, if the "third gender" was inherited and hence, a fixed constant of human variety, the suffering the "concerned persons" underwent, could only be stopped by extending the common understanding of what is natural and the dichotomies of gender. Consequently, he also fought for cancellation of the anti-gay paragraph §175, which was continued in the Weimar Republic, as well as for the right of abortion and contraception and against crude "healing methods" applied to people differing from the norm.

In 1919, Hirschfeld made his dream come true when he established and opened the first Institute of Sexology in Berlin. First of all, this private institution was an academic research centre to investigate so-called sexual malfunctions and an in-house consultation office for problems directly related to sexual identity or sexuality. Frequently, this was the only place where people, who elsewhere would have been criminalized or made psychiatry cases, because of prejudice or doctors' lack of knowledge, could find shelter and help. Contrary to the standards of conventional sexology at the time, Hirschfeld's institute had been dedicated to, "Promote scientific research of the entire sexual life and education in this field." The house, located in the Berlin Tiergarten district, was open to the public, a big difference from many other academic institutes. The museum presented some exhibits from the voluminous and legendary archive, was also open to the public. Regular lectures on sexology took place there as well as training courses for physicians.

This archives housed an unrivalled collection of texts, photos and films, which even in the mere context of consumption, were considered pornography under the law of that time. For the first time, pornography was presented in an academic manner. One of the focal points was homosexuality; others were sado-masochism and fetishism but also trans-identity and cross-dressing of men and women. In 1910, Hirschfeld had already introduced the term of "transvestite" to sexology with his publication "The Transvestites. About the Erotic Urge of Cross-dressing." A popular legend, absolutely unproven however, says Hirschfeld himself visited some of the Berlin cross-dressing houses in his role of "Auntie Magnesia."

Of course, the popularity of Hirschfeld's research was a thorn in the flesh of religious, conservative and fascist ideologists. Even more so, as it simply and logically proved that there are not only the two genders, said to be created by God or nature, in which man dominates woman. In the years between 1919 until it was raided in 1933, the Berlin institute, day by day, collected more evidence against this limited understanding of the world.

In a speech before the Reichstag in 1928, the spokesman of the NSDAP, in a prophecy, defined the line of the future powers: "Those who think of love between man and man, or woman and woman, are our enemies. We will fight everything that emasculates our people and makes it a plaything of its enemies."

The Hirschfeld institute was one of the first institutions the Nazis discredited as vice and they raided and closed it. The institute was raided on May 6, 1933 by students of the Academy of Physical Education and the Veterinary School,

very soon after the National Socialists had taken power. This had a great effect on the media and started the large-scale destruction of humanistic-liberal traditions of thinking, including their political and cultural representatives, by German students.

When people marched, to burn books on the Berlin Opernplatz four days later, "The head of a smashed bust of Magnus Hirschfeld was waved, on a long rod, high above the silent crowds." This was written by German author Erich Kästner, whose books were burned too and was an eyewitness of the debacle. The words illustrate, how Hirschfeld was acquired as a figure of ideological hatred, not only by the Nazis. Under the martial proclamation, "Against over-exaggeration of sexual urges, which splices human souls and pro nobility of the human soul! I herewith dedicate the writings of Sigmund Freud to the flames." Hirschfeld's texts and the biggest part of the archives of the institute were thrown into the flames.

Magnus Hirschfeld died in exile in Nice in 1935. His visionary findings on the variety of human identities were kept hidden, not only during the Nazi dictatorship. They remained suppressed in German academic discourse and gender debates in the decades after 1945. Ironically, it was the indirect continuation of his work by Alfred Kinsey and the Queer Studies in the USA that fuelled a wider interest in Germany in the 1970s, when this aspect of the history of German research and emancipation was taken up once more.

Durch Wissenschaft zur Gerechtigkeit

Magnus Hirschfeld und das Institut für Sexualwissenschaft

Stephanie Kuhnen

„Der Einstein des Sex" war nicht wie zu vermuten wäre der US-amerikanische Sexualforscher und Biologe Alfred Kinsey, sondern der 1868 geborene deutsch-jüdische Arzt Magnus Hirschfeld.
Hirschfeld gilt auch als der Begründer der homosexuellen Emanzipationsbewegung. Selbst homosexuell, gründete er 1897 in Berlin zusammen mit dem Verleger Max Spohr, dem Juristen Eduard Oberg und dem Schriftsteller Max von Bülow das Wissenschaftlich-humanitäre Komitee (WhK), dessen Vorsitz er übernahm. Das Komitee war die weltweit erste Organisation, die sich zum Ziel gesetzt hat, sexuelle Handlungen zwischen Männern zu entkriminalisieren. Sexualität zwischen Frauen war im wilhelminischen Kaiserreich nicht strafbar.
Ab 1899 gab er ein bis 1923 jährlich erschienenes „Jahrbuch für sexuelle Zwischenstufen" heraus. Wie Kinsey Jahrzehnte später in den USA, befragte Hirschfeld ab 1903 zahlreiche Studenten und Metallarbeiter zu ihrer sexuel-

len Orientierung und wertete die Ergebnisse statistisch aus. Nach seinen Erhebungen lag der Anteil Homosexueller an der deutschen Bevölkerung bei 2,3 %, der Bisexueller bei 3,4 %, was zu dieser Zeit einen ungeheuren Skandal darstellte. Im Zuge dessen wurde er von einigen Studenten wegen Beleidigung angezeigt. Als es 1904 zu einer Verurteilung kam, distanzierte sich auch das WhK, obwohl und vielleicht gerade weil es aus vielen homosexuellen Mitgliedern bestand, von Hirschfeld und seiner Befragung.

Hirschfelds Slogan hieß „Durch Wissenschaft zur Gerechtigkeit". Zeitlebens war es sein Hauptanliegen, das Angeborensein von Homosexualität zu beweisen. Von dem deutschen Juristen und Theologen Karl Heinrich Ulrichs (1825 bis 1895) hatte er die Theorie des Dritten Geschlechts, der menschlichen Zwischenstufen, demnach es Homosexuelle, Bisexuelle und Transsexuelle gab, übernommen. Darin unterschied er sich maßgeblich von den populären Theorien des ebenfalls deutsch-österreichischen Psychiaters Richard von Krafft-Ebing (1840 bis 1902) und letztlich auch von Sigmund Freud, die beide Homosexualität als eine Störung der menschlichen Psyche definierten. Der Vorteil seiner Deutung lag für Hirschfeld klar auf der Hand; wenn das „Dritte Geschlecht" ererbt sei und somit eine feste Konstante in der menschlichen Vielfalt darstellte, dann könne das Leid, das den „Betroffenen" u.a. durch Kriminalisierung zugefügt wurde, nur durch eine Erweiterung der gängigen Vorstellung von Natürlichkeit und Geschlechterdichotomien abgestellt werden. Konsequent setzte er sich also für die Aufhebung des auch in der Weimarer Republik weiter bestehenden Anti-Homosexuellen Paragrafen 175, das Recht auf Abtreibung und Verhütung und gegen krude „Heilmethoden" an abweichend von der Norm lebenden Menschen ein.

1919 erfüllte sich Hirschfeld einen Traum mit der Gründung und Eröffnung des ersten Institutes für Sexualwissenschaft in Berlin. In erster Linie war diese private Einrichtung eine wissenschaftliche Forschungsstätte zur Untersuchung von so genannten Sexualstörungen und ambulante Beratungsstelle bei Problemen, die direkt die sexuelle Identität oder die Sexualität betrafen. Oftmals war dies der einzige Ort, an dem Menschen, die sonst aufgrund der Vorur-

teile und des Unwissens der Mediziner kriminalisiert oder psychiatrisiert worden wären, Schutz und Hilfe bekamen. Denn entgegen der Zeitströmung der konventionellen Sexualwissenschaft hatte sich Hirschfelds Institut der „Förderung wissenschaftlicher Forschung des gesamten Sexuallebens und Aufklärung auf diesem Gebiete" verschrieben. Das Haus im Berliner Stadtteil Tiergarten war, anders als viele andere Forschungseinrichtungen, auch der Öffentlichkeit zugänglich, ebenso das Museum, das einige Exponate aus dem umfangreichen wie legendären Archiv ausstellte. Hier fanden regelmäßig Vorträge zur Sexualwissenschaft und Schulungen für Mediziner statt. Dieses Archiv umfasste eine einmalige Sammlung an Schriften, Fotografien und auch Filmen, die im bloßen Konsumkontext nach der damaligen Gesetzgebung als pornografisch galten. Zum ersten Mal wurde auch Pornografie wissenschaftlich aufbereitet. Zu einem der Schwerpunkte gehörten unter anderem Homosexualität, so genannte Paraphilien wie Sadomasochismus und Fetischismus, aber auch Transidentität und männliches wie weibliches Crossdressing. Hirschfeld selbst hatte mit seiner Schrift „Die Transvestiten. Über den erotischen Verkleidungstrieb" bereits 1910 den Begriff des „Transvestiten" in die Sexualwissenschaft eingeführt. Eine beliebte Legende, für die es jedoch keinerlei Belege gibt, besagt, dass Hirschfeld selbst als „Tante Magnesia" in einigen Berliner „Damenimitator"-Lokalen verkehrte.

Selbstverständlich war die Popularität der Hirschfeldschen Forschung den kirchlichen, konservativen und faschistischen Ideologen ein Dorn im Auge, belegte sie doch bestechend einfach und logisch die Unrichtigkeit der angeblich gott- oder naturgegebenen heterosexuellen Zweigeschlecht-

lichkeit, in der der Mann gegenüber der Frau eine Vormachtsstellung genießt. Täglich wurden in den Jahren zwischen 1919 bis zu seiner Plünderung 1933 mehr Gegenbeweise zu diesem Weltbild im Berliner Institut gesammelt.

Der Sprecher der NSDAP legte prophetisch in einer Rede vor dem Reichstag 1928 unmissverständlich die Linie der zukünftigen Machthaber fest: „Wer an Mann-männliche oder Weib-weibliche Liebe denkt, ist unser Feind. Alles, was unser Volk entmannt, zum Spielball seiner Feinde macht, lehnen wir ab."
So war das Hirschfeld-Institut auch eine der ersten Einrichtungen, die von den Nazis als sittenwidrig diskreditiert, geplündert und geschlossen wurden. Die Institutsplünderung am 6. Mai 1933 durch Studenten der Hochschule für

Leibesübungen und der Tierärztlichen Hochschule, verhältnismäßig kurze Zeit nach der Machtergreifung der Nationalsozialisten, stellte den medienwirksam inszenierten Auftakt zur groß angelegten Vernichtung humanistisch-liberaler Denktraditionen einschließlich ihrer politischen und kulturellen Repräsentanten durch die deutsche Studentenschaft dar.
Während des Aufmarschs zur Bücherverbrennung auf dem Berliner Opernplatz vier Tage später schwankte „der Kopf einer zerschlagenen Büste Magnus Hirschfelds [...] auf einer langen Stange [...] hoch über der stummen Menschenmenge". Das schrieb der Schriftsteller Erich Kästner, dessen Bücher ebenfalls verbrannt wurden, als Augenzeuge. Die Worte illustrieren Hirschfelds Indienstnahme als ideologische Hassfigur nicht nur der Nazis. Unter dem Brandspruch „Gegen seelenzerfasernde Überschätzung des Trieblebens, für den Adel der menschlichen Seele! Ich übergebe der Flamme die Schriften von Sigmund Freud" wurden die Schriften Hirschfelds sowie der größte Teil des Institutarchivs auf den Scheiterhaufen geworfen.

Magnus Hirschfeld starb 1935 im Exil in Nizza. Seine vordenkerischen Erkenntnisse um die Vielfalt der menschlichen Identitäten waren nicht nur für die Dauer der nationalsozialistischen Diktatur unsichtbar, sondern blieben auch in den deutschen akademischen Diskursen und Geschlechterdebatten der Jahrzehnte nach 1945 unterdrückt. Ironischerweise bedurfte es der indirekten Fortsetzung seines Wirkens durch Alfred Kinsey und der Queer Studies in den USA, um auch in Deutschland erst in den 1970ern wieder ein größeres Interesse für und eine Anknüpfung an diesen Teil der deutschen Wissenschafts- und Emanzipationsgeschichte zu finden.

RR

D278

Prostitution – the new oldest trade in Germany

Stephanie Kuhnen

Sex work is called the oldest trade on earth with some justification. In the late Renaissance, prostitution was tolerated in Germany in some controlled places. A few bath houses, taverns, brothels were specially marked and a demarcation line – the "Strich" was drawn on the floor. Within the marked area, men and women could work their profession. In order to attract customers, the female sex workers (only heterosexual prostitution was officially permitted) liked to stand on this line called "Strich". Today, the terms "Strichmädchen," "Stricher," or "auf den Strich gehen," are still part of the jargon of this trade in Germany.

The large population growth during the industrial revolution made the number of prostitutes grow rapidly in Germany, in particular in the 19th century. While only few profited from the new wealth, the larger part of the population lived in slums, particularly in the big industrial cities. Women were strongly hit by this tendency, having only little education and insecure jobs. Frequently, only lowly paid jobs were open to them. Most men also earned little.

Women who could make their whole living with sexual services were always a minority. Far more of them had to sell sex in order to make some money, on the side, to support themselves or their families. Spare-time prostitutes included housemaids, factory workers, shop-girls, seamstresses, flower-stall girls and laundry-maids. Many poor families saw no other way but to sell their young daughters and sons as well, to customers via pimps, who charged soliciting fees. At the end of the 19th Century, "wildly spreading prostitution" hiding from state control, was a serious social problem. Men and women worked the trade without any healthcare. Contraception and hygiene were virtually non-existent. Sexually transmitted diseases spread viciously and due to the social origins of the suitors, also slowly reached the middle and upper classes. Considerations of morality and social politics, made the German state see the need to take action. The trade was more and more criminalized, by mass shutdowns of brothels, imprisonment of sex workers and higher punishments for midwives and doctors who did abortions. This forced the concerned persons into social disgrace, more and more and they were without protection from the despotism and cruelty of customers and police. Only a few socially oriented associations and workers' clubs were far-sighted enough to see that only legalisation could stop this misery. There were also the masses of migrants from Eastern Europe, refugees from poverty and political suppression in their own countries, who migrated to the industrial regions of Germany.

Nothing seemed to stop the spread of the sex trade. It had long since exceeded the socially tolerated demarcation line. The blocked areas had spilled over the borders and the trade had become an economy of its own.

Wilhelmian Berlin in 1914 once more tried to establish "controlled tolerance" and distributed 4,000 "control cards" to that number of women who earned their living as so-called "control girls." This helped them avoid prison but they had to undergo monthly health checks.

Under the Prussian law on prostitution, only the verbal offering of sexual services was prohibited but not the actual delivery. Therefore, these women invented new dress codes, to differentiate them from all the normal passersby and to point out their specialties. In Berlin during the Weimar Republic these special insignia, created fashion trends, copied by many young ladies from the upper middle classes. They liked to be considered very chic and turn other peoples' heads. The role of the harlot was very popular in movies and modern art and had a direct affect on fashion and attitudes.For the real sex workers, these quickly changing fashions mainly meant they had to re-invent their appearance over and over.

Indeed, prostitutes in all their forms of appearance were part of the normal street life in Berlin in the Weimar Republic. Up to 120,000 women and up to 35,000 men allegedly, worked the trade in the Republic years before 1933. The large number of different types of prostitutes was unique in Europe. There was nothing that couldn't be had. There was an offer to satisfy every demand. Finding out who would fulfil even the crudest wishes for money and where, was easy. For Berlin citizens and for tourists, the hussies had become a kind of folklore, the muses of street buskers and chansons. Certain urban districts were known for their special types of "professionals."

"Münzi" for instance, were pregnant women awaiting their customers in the Münzstrasse. The most famous hussies were the "Tauentziengirls." Pop culture and art celebrated them with many monuments. They were highly fashionable, with their bobbed haircuts and smoked cigarettes on the streets. They moved around in smaller groups and allowed affluent, mundane gents, who wanted to appear as sponsors rather than customers, "take them out." Most of the girls had quite "honourable" but minor jobs, in order not to compromise their customers too much, when accepting their money for the "relationship." With an estimated number of 2,500 they were very present in the city life of uptown, bourgeois Berlin and the darlings of photographers. The "Chontes" waited for suitors in the Scheunenviertel and all around Alexanderplatz. The Chontes were mainly impoverished East European Jewesses and the most miserable group of the Berlin trade.

Table hostesses, also known as "Berlin Geishas" well into the 1980s, were something very special. In certain houses, they were available for rent together with the table. The "guest" paid a "table fee" to the publican and paid for food and drinks, as well as for the services delivered later, in a nearby hotel room. This escort service was very popular with well-off gents, who expected not only sex, but also more sophisticated conversation. These women were well educated, often fluent in art and literature and in several languages.

Another German slang term was coined by the "Halb-Seiden" or "Semi-Silk" ladies, who seemed to be honourable on the surface, but were indeed not. Today, they would be called "amateur whores;" they also represented the largest

unknown figure on the market. Most of them were amateurs, who earned a little money on the side or perhaps enough for their extravagant lifestyle, attending the many balls at weekends.

As in many other European cities, child prostitution was a profitable, if illegal business. Child prostitutes were known as "phone girls" or "phone boys." They were mainly delivered, to very rich customers, only following a telephone order. The pimps frequently dressed up these early Lolitas like film stars.

The Nazis soon put an end to this colourful and decadent variety. Tolerance in some modern German cities, was superseded by strict and merciless prosecution. Prostitution in all its forms contradicted the politics of the maintenance of the "Pure Race" and was considered a "breeding place of perversion." However, this did not stop the new powers from entertaining their own brothels under their own management. They forced women, who in their racist ideas were considered "non-German" to work for them as whores. Brothels were also entertained in some concentration camps. Women were also forced to serve the "Wehrmacht" in order to "fortify morale." If they were infected with a venereal disease, they were threatened with immediate execution.

Prostitution – das neue älteste Gewerbe in Deutschland

Stephanie Kuhnen

Sexarbeit wird nicht grundlos als das älteste Gewerbe der Welt bezeichnet. Zur Zeit der Spätrenaissance war man in Deutschland dazu übergegangen, Prostitution an einigen kontrollierten Orten zu dulden. Einige Badehäuser, Tavernen und Bordellhäuser wurden speziell gekennzeichnet und auf dem Boden mit einer Trennlinie versehen. Innerhalb dieses Bezirks konnten Frauen wie Männer ihren Geschäften nachgehen. Um Freier anzulocken, standen die Sexarbeiterinnen, denn nur heterosexuelle Prostitution war hier offiziell erlaubt, gerne genau auf diesem Strich. Noch heute sind die Bezeichnungen „Strichmädchen", „Stricher" oder „auf den Strich gehen" fester Jargon.

Aufgrund des starken Bevölkerungswachstums der industriellen Revolution nahm die Zahl der Prostituierten insbesondere im 19. Jahrhundert in Deutschland rasch zu. Während es nur wenige Gewinner des neuen Reichtums gab, stieg die Armut und Verelendung des größten Teils der Menschen vor allem in den Groß- und Industriestädten. Besonders betroffen waren davon Frauen, die meistens nur über eine geringe Ausbildung und unsichere Arbeitsplätze

verfügten und denen häufig nur Tätigkeiten offen standen, in denen sie geringfügige Gehälter verdienten. Da selbst die meisten Männer nur mit wenig Lohn rechnen konnten, blieben die Frauen, die ihren gesamten Lebensunterhalt durch sexuelle Dienstleistungen erwirtschaften konnten immer eine Minderheit gegenüber denjenigen, die sich als Sexarbeiterinnen ein nötiges Zubrot für sich und ihre Familien verdienten. Zu den Gelegenheitsprostituierten zählten Dienstmädchen, Fabrikarbeiterinnen, Verkäuferinnen, Modistinnen, Blumenfrauen und Wäscherinnen. Manche arme Familien sahen sich gezwungen, ihre jungen Töchter und auch Söhne über Zuhälter, die selbstverständlich eine Vermittlungsgebühr einforderten, an Freier zu vermitteln. Gegen Ende des 19. Jahrhunderts stellte die „wild wuchernde Prostitution“, die sich den staatlichen Kontrollen entziehen konnte, ein ernstzunehmendes gesamtgesellschaftliches Problem dar. Die Frauen und Männer arbeiteten ohne jegliche gesundheitliche Versorgung, Verhütungsmittel und Hygiene waren praktisch nicht existent. Neben dem sprunghaften Anstieg von sexuell übertragbaren Krankheiten, die sich allmählich auch aufgrund der sozialen Herkunft der Freier auch in der Mittel- und Oberschicht auszubreiten begannen, führten auch moralische und sozialpolitische Erwägungen dazu, dass man auf staatlicher Seite im Kaiserreich Handlungsbedarf sah. Die verschärfte Kriminalisierung, zum Beispiel durch dic massenhaften Schließungen der Bordelle, Verhaftung der Sexarbeiterinnen, verschärfte Bestrafungen der Abtreibungen vornehmenden Hebammen und Ärzte, trieb die Betroffenen nur immer weiter in die soziale Ächtung und setzte sie schutzlos der Willkür und Gewalt durch Freier und Polizei aus. Nur einige wenige sozialorientierte Vereine und Arbeiterorganisationen besaßen die Weitsicht, dass nur eine Legali-

sierung dem Elend Abhilfe verschaffen könne. Hinzu kamen die Massen an osteuropäischen Migranten, die der Armut oder der politischen Verfolgung in ihren eigenen Ländern zu entkommen versuchten, indem sie in die deutschen Industriegebiete auswanderten.

Nichts schien zu helfen, die Ausbreitung des Sexgewerbes war nicht mehr aufzuhalten. Es hatte die gesellschaftlich geduldete Markierung des Strichs bereits um Meilen überschritten, die Sperrbezirke waren völlig entgrenzt, es hatte sich längst ein eigener Wirtschaftszweig entwickelt.

Im wilhelminischen Berlin 1914 versuchte man sich nochmals an einer „kontrollierten Duldung" und verteilte die auf immerhin 4000 festgesetzte Anzahl von so genannten „Kontrollkarten" an Frauen, die sich als „Kontrollmädchen" ihren Lebensunterhalt verdienten. Dies schützte sie zwar vor Verhaftungen, zwang sie jedoch zur monatlichen Gesundheitskontrolle.

Nach dem preussischen Prostitutionsgesetz war es nur verboten, verbal sexuelle Dienstleistungen anzubieten, nicht aber diese auszuführen. So erfanden die Frauen immer wieder eigene Dresscodes, um sich sowohl von all den normalen Passantinnen zu unterscheiden als auch auf ihre besonderen Spezialitäten hinzuweisen. Besonders im Berlin der Weimarer Zeit entwickelten sich durch diese speziellen Insignien viele modische Trends, die vor allem durch junge Frauen aus der oberen Mittelschicht, die gerne als verrucht und lasterhaft gelten und gesellschaftlich Aufsehen erregen wollten, kopiert wurden. Lottermädchen und mondäne „Girls" wurden auch nicht zuletzt von der in Kinofilmen und moderner Kunst populären Gestalt der „Hure" beeinflusst. Für die tatsächlichen Sexarbeiterinnen bedeuteten diese schnell wechselnden Moden vor allem, ihre Erscheinung ständig neu erfinden zu müssen.

Tatsächlich gehörten Prostituierte in all ihren Erscheinungsformen im Weimarer Berlin zum gewöhnlichen Straßenbild. Angeblich arbeiteten in den Republikjahren bis 1933 bis zu 120.000 Frauen und bis zu 35.000 Männer in diesem Gewerbe. Einmalig in Europa war die Vielfalt der verschiedenen Typen von Prostituierten. Es gab nichts, was es nicht gab. Für jede Nachfrage gab es ein Angebot und man konnte sehr schnell in Erfahrung bringen, wo und wer noch die absonderlichsten Wünsche gegen Geld erfüllte. Für den Berliner und den Touristen waren die Anschafferinnen längst zu einer Art Folklore geworden, der Gassenhauer und Chansons gleichermaßen gewidmet wurden. Ganze Distrikte in der Stadt waren für ihre besonderen „Miezen“ bekannt.

„Münzis“ etwa, waren schwangere Frauen, die in der Münzstrasse auf ihre Kunden warteten. Die berühmtesten, weil ihnen in der Popkultur und Kunst so viele Denkmäler gesetzt wurden, hießen „Tauentziengirls“. Sie gaben sich modisch up-to-date mit Bubikopf und auf der Strasse Zigaretten rauchend, zogen in kleineren Gruppen herum und ließen sich von zahlungskräftigen, mondänen Herren, die sich eher als Gönner denn als Freier verstanden, „ausführen“. Die meisten von ihnen gingen geringfügigen „ehrbaren“ Beschäftigungen nach, auch um ihre Klientel nicht allzu sehr zu kompromittieren, wenn sie sich nach dem „Verhältnis“ Geld zustecken ließen. Mit einer geschätzten Zahl von 2500 waren sie im Straßenbild des gehobenen, bürgerlichen Berlins sehr präsent und die Lieblinge der Fotografen.

Im Scheunenviertel und am Alexanderplatz warteten die Chontes auf ihre Freier. Diese meist osteuropäischen, verarmten Jüdinnen stellten auch die elendste Gruppe des Berliner Gewerbes.

Oft auch die „Berliner Geishas" genannt und noch bis in die 1980er hinein durchaus bekannt, stellten die Tischdamen eine besondere Spezialität dar. Sie konnten in einen speziellen Lokal zusammen mit einem Tisch gemietet werden. Der „Gast" zahlte ein „Tischgeld" beim Wirt und kam für die Verkostung sowie für die anschließenden Dienstleistungen meist in einem nahe gelegenen Hotelzimmer gleich mit auf. Dieser Escort-Service war vor allem bei betuchten Herren von Welt beliebt, da sie nicht nur Sex, sondern auch gehobene Unterhaltung erwarteten. Entsprechend kultiviert waren diese Frauen, viele waren in Kunst und Literatur gebildet und sprachen oft mehrere Sprachen.

Ebenfalls in die deutsche Umgangssprache Einzug hielten die „Halb-Seidenen" also die anscheinend ehrbaren aber unseriösen Damen, heute würden sie „Hobby-Huren" genannt. Sie stellten die zugleich größte Dunkelziffer des Milieus dar. Zumeist waren sie Amateurinnen, die sich an den Wochenenden bei den zahlreichen Tanzveranstaltungen im Anschluss ein Zubrot oder gar einen extravaganten Lebenstil verdienten.

Wie in anderen europäischen Metropolen, war auch die Kinderprostitution ein lukratives wie illegales Geschäft. So genannte „Telephonmädchen" und „Telephonjungs" wurden nur auf Bestellung an ihre zumeist sehr reichen Kunden geliefert. Diese frühen Versionen der Lolita wurden von ihren Zuhältern oft wie Filmstars zurecht gemacht.

Dieser bunten und dekadenten Vielfalt bereiteten die Nazis umgehend ein Ende. Aus der Duldung in einigen modernen deutschen Metropolen folgte eine strikte und gnadenlose Verfolgung. Prostitution in all ihren Erscheinungsformen widersprach der Politik der Erhaltung der „reinen Rasse" und galt als „Brutstätte der Perversion".

Dies hielt die neuen Machthaber aber nicht davon ab, selbst Bordelle unter ihrer Kontrolle zu führen, in denen Frauen, die nach ihren rassistischen Vorstellungen als „undeutsch" galten, gezwungen wurden, als Huren zu arbeiten. In einigen Konzentrationslagern wurden Bordelle geführt. Und auch für die Wehrmacht wurden Frauen zur „Stärkung der Moral" zwangsverpflichtet. Infizierten sie sich mit einer Geschlechtskrankheit, drohte ihnen die sofortige Ermordung.

4
15

4
14

Gay Erotica

Boris von Brauchitsch

In the late 19th century, organised resistance against the §175 was already established. This paragraph made male homosexuality, criminal. The Scientific Humanitarian Committee (WhK) was founded in the Berlin apartment of the young Magnus Hirschfeld (1868-1935) in 1897. The committee started right away to collect signatures for decriminalisation. Regardless of the support by prominent persons, the Reichstag refused the petition in 1898. New hope for liberalization of the anti-homosexual laws did not arise in Germany before the end of the Kaiserreich. However this fragile hope was soon smothered. Although Berlin was a gay Mecca in the 1920s and a very liberal one, the homo-paragraph had not been liberalised. Instead it was considerably aggravated in 1933. Instead of "unnatural sodomy," the offence was now called "sodomy" and "lust-

ful" touching between men was already criminal. Almost one hundred thousand legal suits were opened against gay men between 1933 and 1945. After the end of World War II, some justifiable hope came up that the new democracy might herald the end of persecution of gay people. The first gay bars opened already in 1945 in the allied sectors. But upon the foundation of the two new German states, repression was soon re-enforced. The national authority for publications that might endanger youth "Bundesprüfstelle für jugendgefährdende Schriften" started censoring publications in 1953. Homosexual survivors of concentration camps were not acknowledged as victims. §175, which was maintained in the Nazi version and remained until 1965. It led to almost 45,000 prosecutions and virtually destroyed the lives of those prosecuted.

The activities illustrated in this chapter, have been considered particularly immoral and disgusting and some of them have been real legal risks for the represented persons. Still, the lust in prohibited representation obviously overweighed any concerns. The Catholic Church has always found and still finds, these types of sexuality alarming. Therefore it considers the present legal situation in Germany equal to the Riders of the Apocalypse.

Schwule Erotika

Boris von Brauchitsch

Schon im späten 19. Jahrhundert hatte sich ein organisierter Widerstand gegen den seit 1871 geltenden § 175 formiert, der männliche Homosexualität unter Strafe stellte. In der Berliner Wohnung des jungen Magnus Hirschfeld (1868-1935) gründete sich 1897 das Wissenschaftlich-humanitäre Komitee (WhK), dass sofort damit begann, Unterschriften für eine Entkriminalisierung zu sammeln. Obwohl Prominente das Vorhaben unterstützten, lehnte der Reichstag 1898 die Petition ab, und erst mit dem Ende des Kaiserreichs keimte in Deutschland neue Hoffnung für eine Liberalisierung der anti-homosexuellen Gesetze auf, die allerdings bald schon gedämpft werden sollte. Auch wenn Berlin in den 20er Jahren das Mekka der Schwulen war und eine ausgesprochene Freizügigkeit herrschte, kam es nicht mehr zu einer Liberalisierung des Homoparagraphen, der 1933 sofort deutlich verschärft wurde. Statt „widernatürli-

cher Unzucht“ hieß es nun allgemein „Unzucht“, was auch „wollüstige“ Berührungen zwischen Männern bereits unter Strafe stellte. Rund hunderttausend Verfahren gegen Schwule wurden zwischen 1933 und 1945 eingeleitet. Nach Kriegsende keimte einmal mehr berechtigte Hoffnung auf, dass nun mit der neuen Demokratie auch die Verfolgung der Homosexuellen enden könnte. Erste schwule Lokale eröffneten bereits 1945 in den Sektoren der Alliierten, doch mit Gründung der beiden deutschen Staaten setzten auch die Repressalien wieder verstärkt ein. Die Bundesprüfstelle für jugendgefährdende Schriften zensierte ab 1953 Publikationen, den homosexuellen KZ-Insassen wurde jede Anerkennung als Opfer verweigert und der Paragraph 175, der in seiner NS-Fassung beibehalten wurde, führte bis 1965 in Deutschland zu rund 45.000 Verurteilungen, die Existenzvernichtungen gleichkamen.

Die Praktiken, die auf den Bildern dieses Kapitels zu sehen sind, waren also durchgehend moralisch besonders verwerflich und zumindest teilweise auch ein echtes juristisches Risiko für die Dargestellten. Dennoch hat sich offenbar die Lust an der verbotenen Darstellung immer wieder klar gegen mögliche Bedenken durchgesetzt. Besonders für die katholische Kirche waren diese Spielarten ohnehin damals wie heute ein alarmierendes Zeichen. Die gegenwärtige Gesetzeslage in Deutschland erscheint ihr denn auch zwangsläufig als Vorbote der Apokalypse.

Lesbian Love

Stephanie Kuhnen

Until today, representation of women having sex with women is a major segment of pornography. Such pictures however, are produced mainly by heterosexual men.

The term "lesbian love" appeared in a German encyclopaedia for the first time in 1787. Fifty years later, the German standard encyclopaedia Brockhaus, for the first time refers to "Sapphian Love," relating to the classical poet and teacher Sappho, who was said to have maintained love relations with her female pupils on the Greek island of Lesbos. Originally, "lesbian" meant only cunnilingus between women. Only after the rise of sexology in the 19th century, was the image of lesbian women as known today, developed. These studies and considerations have been made exclusively, by male scientists. Hence, they also manifested definitions that had little to do with the real experience and

lifestyle of lesbian women; they came rather from imagination, than from reality.

Pornographic fantasies about women without men were very popular in the pornographic folklore art, at least since the political satires of the Reformation Age. For instance, these illustrations were meant to dishonour the life of nuns in cloisters and at the same time, the very explicit illustrations were meant to sexually stimulate the beholder. More topics were added in the 18th century, for instance, horny ladies of the gentry, who obliged their chambermaids to render sexual services. The first pornographic photos also included illustrations of female couples in different sexual activities. They frequently performed them for an imaginary beholder, directly looking into the camera. Actually, these photos were often taken by amateur photographers, in a brothel, with prostitutes, for private use. Some of the very explicit illustrations show women having sex with a dildo belt, a utensil some prostitutes offered to heterosexual customers as a special extra. This happened in a rather sadomasochistic environment and was taboo.

The "Phallic Woman" as she was called in the early sexology of the late 19th century, was also a demonic seducer, who drew "honourable girls" down into the gutter with her "sick" appetite and finally ruined them. This decadent vision was very popular into the 1920s, as it was in established art and literature and not only in Germany since it reflected very present worries. The industrial revolution and the structural changes in society had clearly rung in the end of the undisputed dominance of men over women. The "rule of wives" and "women with male characteristics" were turned into freak ghosts as well as erotic stimuli.

Lesbian women did not become visible in society or the media until the Weimar Republic. Of course, this development was not very sudden and it was no coincidence that it coincided with the set-up of the republic. It was a result of the generally modified position of women in society.

At the turn of the century, the first women's liberation movement had taken a very vocal part in social discourse. Women had become a part of public life, even without male companions. These and other emancipation trends created a new understanding of sexuality, individuality and morality in the population. Leisure was democratized and finally also eroticized. Germans were now able to go on holiday or undertake new leisure activities after work, such as partaking in cultural events or a night on the town, go to dances and fall in love. In the big cities, amusement bars shot up like mushroom on wet wood. They attracted guests, with stimulating promotions and exotic music. There was an attempt to cater for every need. Not least, lesbian women benefitted from the gay movement, which grew stronger and stronger. However female homosexuality was not a crime, as was male homosexuality. Therefore, lesbian subculture had a great advantage and it was easier for lesbians to appear in public. Artists and journalists were fascinated by the "New Women." Many paintings, photos and literary texts today, still bear witness to the popularity, which could never be restored after 1933. For actresses of the time, it was even a career plus when there was at least suspicion of a liaison with another actress. As today, in the gay subculture, lesbian women were considered trendsetters in fashion. Their setting between the genders, their appropriation of male encoded accessories and short haircuts were gladly taken over and copied by the mainstream. Being lesbian was "in", even if women only played at it.

The new liberty of the press and the energy of a young political and cultural movement, created in Germany, a large number of successful women's magazine with great circulations. For instance, "Die Freundin" or "Garconne," created platforms for lesbians to discuss their interests. Further to articles on style and daily events, prepared for the target group of lesbians and photo series, literary writing and event reports were the most important contents. Sexual matters were addressed quite openly for that time. The independent erotic lifestyle was still new and tried to find a special language for lesbian demands and to think female sexuality without male sexuality. Today we might wonder how obviously lesbian sexuality was visible in public, in all its diversity. In a rather short time, a wide-ranging and colourful erotic literature from lesbians, for lesbians, was created from 1922 until the prohibition of all homosexual magazines by the Nazis. Hardly begun, it had to disappear again from the scene. "Lesbian Porn" on the other hand, for a male heterosexual audience, fell under the general ban on pornography under the Nazis, but because of the rather "harmless" content, it was tolerated more than gay pornography, possession of which could be punished with deportation to a work camp.

In Germany, lesbian women did not take up the representation of their sexuality, in their own hands before the 1990s.

Lesbische Liebe

Stephanie Kuhnen

Bis heute nimmt die Darstellung von Frauen, die miteinander Sex haben, einen großen Bereich in der Pornographie ein. Produziert und konsumiert werden diese Bilder aber zur großen Mehrheit von heterosexuellen Männern.

Der Begriff „lesbische Liebe" taucht erstmals in einem deutschen Lexikon 1787 auf. Fünfzig Jahre später referiert das deutsche Standardlexikon Brockhaus erstmals auf die „sapphische Liebe" und stellt damit den Bezug zu der antiken Dichterin und Erzieherin Sappho her, die auf der griechischen Insel Lesbos analog zum üblichen mann-männlichen pädagogischen Eros Liebesbeziehungen zu ihren Schülerinnen unterhalten haben soll. Ursprünglich bezeichnete „lesbisch" vorwiegend nur den Cunnilingus unter Frauen. Erst durch die Sexualwissenschaften des 19. Jahrhunderts wurde das noch heute gültige Bild von lesbischen Frauen geprägt. Da diese Untersuchungen und Über-

legungen ausschließlich von männlichen Wissenschaftlern gemacht wurden, manifestierten sich damit auch Definitionen, die mit dem tatsächlichen Erleben und den Lebensentwürfen von Lesben wenig zu tun hatten und eher der Fantasie als der Realität entsprungen sind.

Pornografische Fantasien über Frauen, die ohne einen Mann auszukommen gezwungen waren, erreichten in der pornografischen Volkskunst dagegen spätestens seit den politischen Satiren der Reformationszeit einen hohen Verbreitungsgrad. So sollten darin zum Beispiel die Lebensweise von Nonnen in den Klöstern diffamiert und sich gleichzeitig an den sehr expliziten Darstellungen von Frauen angeregt werden. Mit dem 18. Jahrhundert kamen verschiedene Topoi hinzu wie beispielsweise lüsterne adelige Frauen, die ihre Mägde auch zu sexuellen Dienstleistungen verpflichteten. Mit dem 19. Jahrhundert stellte die gesellschaftskritische Ebene nur noch eine Option dar. Zu den ersten pornographischen Fotografien gehörten auch Abbildungen von Frauenpaaren bei unterschiedlichen sexuellen Handlungen, die sie oft für einen imaginierten Betrachter mit direktem Blick in die Kamera aufführten. Tatsächlich wurden diese auch oft von Amateurfotografen nur für ein kleines Publikum in einem Bordell mit Prostituierten aufgenommen. Einige der besonders expliziten Aufnahmen zeigten Frauen beim Sex mit einem Umschnalldildo, einem Utensil, das einige Prostituierte als besondere Delikatesse für heterosexuelle Freier anboten, dies aber eher in einem sadomasochistischen Zusammenhang und entsprechend tabuisiert.

Die „phallische Frau“, wie sie in den frühen Sexualwissenschaften des späten 19. Jahrhunderts genannt wurde, war auch dämonische Verführerin, die „anständige Mäd-

chen“ mit ihrem „kranken“ sexuellen Appetit in den Abgrund zog und sie zu ihresgleichen machte. Diese Dekadenzmetapher war bis in die 1920er Jahre auch in der etablierten Kunst und Literatur nicht nur in Deutschland äußerst beliebt, da sie sehr präsente Ängste reflektierte. Durch die industrielle Revolution und die gesamtgesellschaftlichen strukturellen Veränderungen, war das Ende der unangefochtenen Vormachtstellung der Männer gegenüber den Frauen unmissverständlich eingeleitet worden. „Die Weiberherrschaft“ sowie „die Vermännlichung der Frauen“ wurde zum Schreckgespenst und erotischem Anheizer gleichermaßen.

Lesbische Frauen selbst wurden erst mit der Weimarer Republik in der Öffentlichkeit und in den Medien sichtbar. Diese Entwicklung ging selbstverständlich nicht schlagartig und nicht erst mit Republikgründung vonstatten. Letztlich war sie ein Ergebnis der allgemein veränderten Stellung der Frau.

Bereits um die Jahrhundertwende hatte sich die erste Frauenbewegung unübersehbar in gesellschaftliche Diskurse eingemischt. Frauen waren nun auch ohne legitime männliche Begleitung Teil des öffentlichen Lebens. Diese und andere emanzipatorische Strömungen schufen in der Bevölkerung ein neues Verständnis von Sexualität, Individuum und Moral. Zudem wurde „Freizeit“ demokratisiert und letztlich auch erotisiert. Jeder und jede Deutsche konnte nun in die Ferien fahren oder nach getaner Arbeit den neuen Freizeitaktivitäten nachgehen wie zum Beispiel an kulturellen Ereignissen teilnehmen, sich zu einem Bummel durch die Stadt verabreden, Tanzveranstaltungen besuchen und sich dort verlieben. In den Großstädten schossen

die Vergnügungslokale wie Pilze aus dem Boden, lockten mit aufreizender Werbung und „exotischer Musik". Für jede Zielgruppe gab es auch ein Angebot. Nicht zuletzt profitierten lesbische Frauen auch von der immer stärker werdenden Schwulenbewegung. Da weibliche Homosexualität im Gegensatz zu männlicher aber nicht unter Strafe stand, hatte die lesbische Subkultur zudem eine deutlichen Vorteil und Lesben konnten sich auch als Einzelpersonen leichter in der Öffentlichkeit zeigen. Künstler und Journalisten reagierten fasziniert von diesen „neuen Frauen". Zahlreiche Gemälde, Fotografien und literarische Texte zeugen noch heute von einer Popularität, wie sie nach 1933 nie wieder entstehen konnte. Es galt für Schauspielerinnen dieser Zeit sogar als besonders Karriere fördernd, wenn ihnen zumindest eine Liaison mit einer Kollegin nachgesagt werden konnte. Wie heute noch die schwule Subkultur, galten lesbische Frauen auch in Modefragen als Trendsetterinnen. Ihre Inszenierungen zwischen den Geschlechtern, ihre Aneignung männlich kodierter Accessoires und Kurzhaarschnitte wurden gerne vom so genannten Mainstream übernommen und kopiert. Lesbischsein war „in", auch wenn damit nur kokettiert wurde.

Mit der neu gewonnenen Pressefreiheit und dem ganzen Elan einer jungen politischen und kulturellen Bewegung, entstand in Deutschland eine große Vielfalt an erfolgreichen und auflagenstarken Frauenmagazinen wie „Die Freundin" oder „Garçonne", in denen Lesben ihre Belange diskutieren konnten. Neben Artikeln, die Stilfragen und Tagesgeschehen für die Leserinnen zielgruppengerecht aufbereiteten und Fotostrecken, stellten literarische Texte und Erlebnisberichte einen großen Teil des Inhalts. Für ihre Zeit wurden vor allem Fragen der Sexualität offen ausgesprochen. Die eigenständige, erotische Lebensweise war noch

neu und dementsprechend war man bemüht, eine eigene Sprache für das lesbische Begehren zu entwickeln, überhaupt weibliche Sexualität ohne die männliche zu denken. Heute mag es verblüffen, wie deutlich lesbische Sexualität in aller Diversität öffentlich sichtbar war. In verhältnismäßig kurzer Zeit, von 1922 bis zum Verbot aller homosexuellen Zeitschriften durch die Nazis, entstand eine umfangreiche wie bunte erotische Literaturgeschichte von Lesben für Lesben, die, kaum entwickelt, bereits wieder von der Bildfläche verschwinden musste.

„Lesbenporno" für ein heterosexuelles, männliches Publikum dagegen fiel zwar unter das allgemeine Pornografieverbot der Nazis, war aber wegen seines „harmlosen Inhalts" eher geduldet als schwule Pornografie, deren Besitz bereits mit Deportation in ein Arbeitslager bestraft werden konnte.

Lesbische Frauen selbst nahmen in Deutschland die Darstellung ihrer Sexualität erst wieder in den 1990ern in die eigene Hand.

Ethnographic nude photography

Nude photography or science

The editor

Considering how difficult photography was at the end of the 19th century, with big, heavy cameras, long illumination times, fragile glass plates and so on, the incredible masses of preserved, ethnographic photos are amazing. The Berlin association of anthropology, ethnology and pre-history (Berliner Gesellschaft für Anthropologie, Ethnologie und Urgeschichte) alone, possessed more than 20,000 photos in 1939.

A large number of these photographic documents on ethnic people was taken for science and research, and used mainly for measuring, categorizing and listing. Many other photos, mainly those with erotic attraction, were often used for financing the expeditions. Books and magazines under titles such as "Woman in the Life of People" or "Racial Beauty of Woman" were a way, in the sexually inhibited Kaiserreich, to satisfy the educated upper classes with voyeuristic literature, all clandestine under the academic gown.

Ethnografische Aktfotografie

Aktfotografie oder Wissenschaft

Der Herausgeber

Wenn man weiß, wie beschwerlich das Fotografieren am Ende des 19. Jahrhunderts war – dicke schwere Kameras, lange Belichtungszeiten, zerbrechliche Glasträger usw. – ist die unglaubliche Menge an überlieferten „ethnografischen" Fotografien kaum vorstellbar. Allein die Berliner Gesellschaft für Anthropologie, Ethnologie und Urgeschichte besaß 1939 über 20.000 Fotografien.

Ein Großteil dieser fotografischen Dokumente über Urvölker diente damals der Wissenschaft, und wurde vornehmlich zum Vermessen, Kategorisieren und Katalogisieren genutzt. Ein anderer großer Teil der Fotos, vor allem die mit erotischer Ausstrahlung, wurde oft zur Finanzierung der Expeditionsreisen verwendet. In Büchern und Zeitschriften mit Titeln wie „Das Weib im Leben der Völker" oder „Rassenschönheit des Weibes" wurde in der sexuell gehemmten Kaiserzeit eine Möglichkeit gefunden, das gebildete Bürgertum mit voyeuristischer Literatur zu befriedigen – alles unter dem Deckmantel der Wissenschaft.

Attraction and power of the Exotic

Boris von Brauchitsch

Being fascinated by what is different is a constant of human behaviour. This is why the relationship to the residents of Africa was a central issue in Western Culture. Normally, racism was maintained to confirm the superiority of the Europeans. Figures such as the Negro Monostratos in Mozart's "Zauberflöte" - The Magic Flute (this title has a subtle connotation in the erotic context) manifested the typical image of black people. The sexually greedy, palace guardsman approaches the white beauty, being aware that "a black man is ugly." Noble cultivation is opposed to the elementary urge: "Weiss ist schön, ich muss es küssen – sollt' es dich zu sehr verdrießen, oh so mach die Augen zu." (White is beautiful, I have to kiss her – if you mind, close your eyes…)

A more positively coloured version of this racism was found in the enthusiasm of expressionists at the beginning of the 20th century, who considered the alleged "primitivism" of African culture as a soothing balm to the burnt-out European decadence.

Exploring foreign continents and conquering them by photography became the fashion already in the second half of the 19th Century. Photos of naked people in Africa and

Asia were very widespread. The underlying motif was not only academic research and humanistic thinking but also the idea that knowledge of foreign cultures was the most important impulse to understand and tolerate them. Voyeurism was also an important drive. On the one hand, erotica was sold under the cover of ethnological studies. On the other hand, the myth of the wild black man was maintained, who with his alleged great libido still had something of the animal. "Real men" and "tribal mothers" were represented and their natural ways promised excitement and stimulation of a very special kind.

At the turn of the 19th Century, more and more news of unrest in the colonies reached Europe. Few Europeans might have expected gratefulness for their Imperialism. However they had not expected the growing resistance, which could no longer be ignored. In this climate of cruelty and conflict, the thought of the physical and sexual superiority of the black, entered thoughts and photos. The revenge of the black man for centuries of oppression. Once unleashed, he would not refrain from conquering white woman, who – as seen in the illustration – does not really try to get out of his arms.

Reiz und Gewalt der Exotic

Boris von Brauchitsch

Die Faszination durch das Andersartige ist eine menschliche Verhaltenskonstante. Ein zentrales Thema im abendländischen Kulturkreis blieb dementsprechend das Verhältnis zu den Bewohnern Afrikas. Üblicherweise wurde ein Rassismus gepflegt, der die Überlegenheit der Europäer konstatierte und in Figuren wie dem Mohr Monostratos in Mozarts „Zauberflöte“ (der Titel bekommt im Erotik-Kontext noch einmal eine ganz andere Note) das typische Schwarzen-Bild festschrieb. Der sexuell gierige Palastwächter nähert sich der weißen Schönheit im Bewusstsein, dass „ein Schwarzer hässlich ist“. Edle Kultiviertheit steht hier gegen elementaren Trieb: „Weiß ist schön, ich muss es küssen – sollt‘ es dich zu sehr verdrießen, oh so mach die Augen zu...“. Eine positiv gefärbte Variante dieses Rassismus liefert die Begeisterung des Expressionismus zu Beginn des 20. Jahrhunderts, die die vermeintliche „Primitivität“ der afrikanischen Kultur als wohltuenden Kontrast zur ausgebrannten Dekadenz Europas empfand.

Die Erkundung fremder Kontinente und ihre fotografische Besitzergreifung kam bereits in der zweiten Hälfte des 19. Jahrhunderts in Mode. Eine besondere Bandbreite liefern die Fotografien von Nacktheit in Afrika und Asien. Dabei ging es nicht nur um wissenschaftliche Erkenntnis und

humanistische Vorstellungen, die im Wissen über fremde Kulturen den wichtigsten Impuls für Verständnis und Toleranz sahen, sondern auch um Voyeurismus. Zum einen wird unter dem Deckmantel ethnologischer Studien Erotik verkauft, zum andern wird der Mythos vom wilden Schwarzen bedient, der sich nicht zuletzt durch seine angeblich besonders ausgeprägte Libido das Animalische bewahrt hat. Hier werden uns „richtige Männer“ und „Urmütter“ vorgeführt, deren Natürlichkeit eine Auf- und Erregung der besonderen Art verspricht.
Um die Wende des 19. zum 20. Jahrhunderts drangen zunehmend Nachrichten von Unruhen in den Kolonien nach Europa. Dankbarkeit für ihren Imperialismus hatten wohl die wenigsten Europäer erwartet, aber dass sich doch nach und nach ein Widerstand formierte, der nicht mehr zu ignorieren war, bereitete auch ihnen Sorge. In diesem Klima der Gewalt fand sich auch der Gedanke der physischen und sexuellen Überlegenheit der Schwarzen in den Köpfen und in Fotografien ein: die Revanche des schwarzen Mannes für jahrhunderte lange Unterdrückung. Einmal entfesselt scheut er sich nicht vor der Besitzergreifung der weißen Frau, die sich – wie in den hier gezeigten Abbildung – allerdings auch nur recht halbherzig seinem Griff zu entziehen versucht.

German Nude Culture

Stephanie Kuhnen

Ever since classical times, the Germans had been known for roaming the countryside stark naked, as described by Roman poet Tacitus. Indeed, it had been customary in all of Central Europe to bathe in the nude, if separated by gender.

Only when nakedness was made taboo, and thus sexualized, natural naked behaviour started to disappear. Surely the growing density of population also played a part. Dress codes could never be enforced in scarcely populated Scandinavia. Therefore, "bathing Swedish" for bathing in the nude had been a popular slang term.

Especially in regions with mainly working class population, such as the Ruhr area or the Rhineland, but also in the traditionally, slightly more liberal Prussia, opposition against the morals of the Christian bourgeoisie began to grow, at least with regards to dress codes. The slogan was

"Being naked and right-doing is much better than being dressed up but embarrassed and ashamed of one's own body". The majority of the supporters of "natural nakedness" were politically rather left-wing, and they emphasized the "natural equality of all people."

At the end of the 19th Century, Berlin already became the centre of the organized, reform-oriented "Lichtkleid-Freunde" and "Wandervögel." There, among the dark bakkyards, which were cold even in summer, dirty factory halls, rotten roads and bitter poverty, the longing for sun, fresh air, and to overcome class barriers seemed at its greatest. First, nudists were observed with mistrust by the Wilhelmian guards of morality, and punished with special restrictions. With the set-up of the Weimar Republic, and the simultaneous loosening of the conventional rules, this seemingly immoral extravagance of youth, intellectuals and the working class was becoming more and more accepted in public. All over Germany and Austria, nude culture clubs came up, with very different political lines. They had great names such as "Freisonnlandbund," "Bund der Lichtfreunde" or "Deutsche Luftbadegesellschaft." "Naked and Free" was a slogan as modern as Women's Lib, Charleston and Bauhaus. Only the representatives of the Catholic Church and the Christian parties seemed to mind. Their moral dislike was opposed by more and more magazines for nude activists, who confronted their enemy, the prudish Philistines. This was made possible by the new, democratic liberty of print media. The distribution of image materials however, still had to pass the censor. Every volume of the magazines was in danger of being seized for distribution of "obscene materials." However, this became less frequent, the more the young republic established its democratic role.

Each of the magazines followed its own political opinion. Most tied the naked body to the ideological goals of their publishers. In these fields, more emphasis was put on the representation of one's own philosophies than on independent journalism. One of the magazines with the greatest circulation was "Die Freude," a monthly magazine, which represented socialist and nationalist ideas and related to expressionism in its design. "Das Freibad" presented itself non-political and hedonistic. Magnus Hirschfeld and Maria Krische of the Institute of Sexology published the most advanced magazine, "Die Aufklärung." This magazine was designed in Bauhaus style and dealt with sexual political issues, hygiene questions, anthropological and historical essays. It was the only magazine that was open to homosexual or transsexual lifestyles. Very early, magazines popped up, for example the papers "Kraft und Schönheit," "Lichtland" and "Der Leib" that were close to racist ideas of the national socialists and tied natural romanticism with antisemitism and a population policy of "racial purity." Of course, the wake of the flood of magazines also gave room for irregular publications which were more "image oriented" and tried to overcome the accusation of being pornographic by adding a little text.

All these publications, whether rather leftwing or rightwing in politics, were founded with the intention of creating a new, more liberal society, in which all people would be equal by birth and sexually enlightened. Exploding capitalism brought a few liberties for the Germans. The majority however, had to face new and threatening consequences: poverty, insecure assets and employment, hunger, illnesses, prostitution, criminality, environmental pollution and ever growing birth rates of single young women. Sunbathing in

the nude despite great inflation seemed to take everyday sorrow away from the Germans, at least for a short moment.

In 1931, Berlin alone maintained more than 40 associations and clubs for "nude culture". Figures for all of Germany are contradictory, as clubs seemed to be founded, split, dissolved, merged and fused or shattered all the time.

When the National Socialists took over power in 1933, and started right away to implement their ideologies, they were faced with a hardly organized mass movement with many supporters, who might have become a factor of insecurity for the new regime any time.

The new powers made good use of the overlap between their ideas of a "new society" and those of the life reformers, integrating them into their own plans. The latent, rather romantic ideas of a pre-Christian or Heathen "Nordic People," where women, men and children were healthy and merry and frolicked around on green meadows, were merged with some skill with the racist fiction of an "Arian Race," which was to be purified of all "Jewish rottenness," "unhealthy life" and "Christian puritan compulsion" and to ring in the "New Age" of the "Supreme Race". All publications and clubs that opposed these ideas, or didn't want to consolidate, were forbidden. It was this movement, the German nude culture annexed and redefined by the NSDAP that was later used to illustrate and prove the "moral perversion" of the Nazis by the Catholic Church, when it tried to restore its power after the war in Western Germany. Through the fifties and sixties, it was a special attention of the guardians of morals, in church or close to church, to maintain the ban on all publications of the life reformers. Efforts to revive some of the magazines were soon beaten down with

regularity. Stalls selling them went up in flames. Bookshops were sued for the distribution of pornography. Print shops refused to print them for fear of losing other orders. This censoring was not greatly opposed, for one reason: the Germans had their hands full with building up their country and with simple survival. Indeed, the Christian conservative and anti-socialist forces won so much ground in the Federal Republic of Germany that it was not until the left-wing student movement of 1968 and the parallel sexual liberalization that the naked body itself, was no longer considered pornographic. Only then a new, if non-political, nude culture cropped up, once more in the West.

Things were different for German sunbathers in the GDR (Eastern Germany), set-up in 1949. For pure opposition against the conservative west, and with reference to the historic working-class roots of the naturalist movement and their idea of equality of man, the socialist government tolerated nude bathing at most lakes and beaches, although strongly controlled and ruled. Today, 20 years after the re-unification, most of the nude beaches and lakes are still on the territory of the former GDR. Some regions even mark, not the beach sections where nude bathing is permitted, but the areas where visitors are obliged to wear clothes. The "textile" beach shows that the clothed, German sun lover is still a minority on this territory.

Auf dem alten Gelände 1931

Auf dem Gelände, Sommer 1932

Auf dem Gelände August 1932

Die Deutsche Nacktkultur

Stephanie Kuhnen

Schon in der Antike waren die Germanen dank des römischen Dichters Tacitus dafür bekannt, sich bei jeder Gelegenheit gerne nackt durch die Natur zu bewegen. Tatsächlich war es in ganz Mitteleuropa bis ins späte 18. Jahrhundert noch üblich, wenn auch getrennt nach Geschlechtern, nackt zu baden.

Erst durch die Tabuisierung und letztlich Sexualisierung des Nacktseins an sich, verschwand der natürliche Umgang mit dem unbedeckten Körper. Sicherlich spielte auch die zunehmende Bevölkerungsdichte eine Rolle: in den skandinavischen Ländern konnten Bekleidungspflichten nie durchgesetzt werden. Im Volksmund sprach man daher auch von „Schwedisch-Baden", wenn man „nackt Baden" meinte.

Vor allem in Regionen mit stark proletarisch ausgerichteter Bevölkerung wie dem Ruhrgebiet und dem Rheinland, aber auch im traditionell etwas liberaleren Preußen, formierte sich ab Mitte des 19. Jahrhunderts eine Opposition

gegen die Moralvorstellungen des christlichen Bürgertums, zumindest was die Kleiderordnung betraf. Das Motto war: „Nackt und umgeben mit Rechtschaffenheit zu sein, ist weitaus besser, als prächtig gekleidet und geplagt durch Scham vor dem Körper." So stand die Mehrheit der Anhänger der „natürlichen Nacktheit" politisch auch eher links und betonte die „natürliche Gleichheit aller Menschen".

Berlin wurde bereits gegen Ende des 19. Jahrhunderts Zentrum der organisierten und reformerisch orientierten „Lichtkleid-Freunde" und „Wandervögel". Dort, zwischen dunklen und auch im Sommer kalten Hinterhöfen, schmutzigen Fabrikhallen, dreckigen Straßen und bitterer Armut schien die Sehnsucht nach Sonne, frischer Luft und Überwindung der Klassengesellschaft am größten. Zunächst noch von den wilhelminischen Sittenwächtern argwöhnisch beobachtet und mit allerlei Sonderauflagen schikaniert, erfreute sich diese scheinbar unmoralische Extravaganz der Jugend, der Intellektuellen und der Arbeiterschicht spätestens mit Gründung der Weimarer Republik und der damit einhergehenden Lockerung der Versammlungsgesetze zunehmender öffentlicher Akzeptanz. Überall in Deutschland und Österreich entstanden Freikörpervereine unterschiedlichster politischer Ausrichtungen. Sie trugen klangvolle Namen wie „Freisonnlandbund", „Bund der Lichtfreunde" oder „Deutsche Luftbadegesellschaft". „Nackt und frei" war als Motto modern wie Frauenwahlrecht, Charleston und Bauhaus. Daran störten sich fast nur noch die katholischen Kirchenvertreter sowie die christlichen Parteien. Ihrer moralischen Entrüstung traten nun immer zahlreicher erscheinende Magazine für die Nacktaktivisten entgegen, die sich ihrerseits an dem Feindbild des prüden Spießers abarbeiteten. Die neue, demokratische

Pressefreiheit machte es möglich. Einzig mit der Verbreitung von Bildmaterial tat sich der Zensor noch schwer, und jede Ausgabe der Zeitschriften lief immer wieder Gefahr, wegen Verbreitung „obszönen Materials“ beschlagnahmt zu werden. Dies geschah allerdings immer weniger häufig, je mehr sich die junge Republik als Demokratie festigen konnte.

Jedes Magazin verfolgte seine eigene politische Weltanschauung. Die meisten verbanden den nackten Körper mit den ideologischen Zielen ihrer Herausgeber, da in diesem

Themengebiet mehr Wert auf die Darstellung der eigenen Philosophien als auf unabhängigen Journalismus gelegt wurde. Zu den auflagenstärksten Publikationen zählte „Die Freude“, ein monatliches Magazin, das sozialistische und nationalistische Ansichten vertrat und gestalterisch dem Expressionismus verbunden war. „Das Freibad“ gab sich apolitisch und hedonistisch. Das fortschrittlichste Magazin, „Die Aufklärung“, wurde von Magnus Hirschfeld und Maria Krishe vom Institut für Sexualwissenschaft herausgegeben. In diesem nach Bauhaus-Stil gestaltetem Magazin befasste man sich mit sexualpolitischen Themen, Hygienefragen, anthropologischen und historischen Aufsätzen und gab sich als einziges aufgeschlossen gegenüber homo- und transsexuellen Lebensstilen. Sehr früh entstanden aber auch Magazine, wie zum Beispiel die Zeitschriften „Kraft und Schönheit“, „Lichtland“ und „Der Leib“, die den rassistischen Ideen der Nationalsozialisten nahe standen, indem sie Naturromantik mit Antisemitismus und einer „artreinen“ Bevölkerungspolitik verknüpften. Selbstverständlich wurden im Kielwasser der Magazinflut auch unregelmäßige Publikationen veröffentlicht, die sich „bildorientiert“ gaben und sich mit wenig Text dem Vorwurf der Pornografie zu entziehen versuchten.

Allen diesen Publikationen, waren sie nun politisch eher links oder eher rechts zuzuordnen, lag das Anliegen zu Grunde, eine neue, freiheitlichere Gesellschaft zu schaffen, in der alle Menschen von Geburt gleich und sexuell aufgeklärt sind.

Der explodierende Kapitalismus brachte zwar für die Deutschen einige wenige Freiheiten mit sich. Die Mehrheit jedoch sah sich vor allem völlig neuen bedrohlichen Konsequenzen ausgesetzt: Armut, unsichere Vermögens- und

Beschäftigungsverhältnisse, Hunger, Krankheiten, Prostitution, Kriminalität, Umweltverschmutzung, eine ständig ansteigende Geburtenrate bei unverheirateten jungen Frauen. Sich nach der großen Inflation nackt in die Sonne zu legen, nahm dem Deutschen für einen kurzen Moment die täglichen Sorgen des Alltags.

1931 gab es allein in Berlin über 40 Gesellschaften und Vereine für „Nacktkultur". Für ganz Deutschland sind die Zahlen widersprüchlich, da ständig neue Vereine gegründet, aufgelöst, in Dachverbänden eingeschmolzen wurden oder in Splittergruppen zerfielen.

Als die Nationalsozialisten 1933 die Macht übernahmen und sofort begannen, ihre Ideologien umzusetzen, trafen sie auf eine wirr organisierte Massenbewegung mit vielen Sympathisanten, die jederzeit zu einem unkontrollierbaren Unsicherheitsfaktor für das neue Regime hätte werden können.

Die neuen Machthaber machten sich die Überschneidungen ihrer Vorstellungen von einer „neuen Gesellschaft" mit denen der Lebensreformer geschickt zu Nutze, um diese in die eigenen Pläne einzubinden. Vorher latent vorhandene, eher romantische Ideen von einem vorchristlich-heidnischen „nordischen Volk", das gesund und fröhlich, Frauen, Männer, Kinder Seite an Seite über die Wiesen tollend Leibesübungen nachgeht, wurden geschickt verwoben mit der rassistischen Fiktion einer „arischen Rasse", die rein von aller „jüdischen Verderbtheit", „ungesundem Leben" und „christlich puritanischem Zwang" das „neue Zeitalter" der „Herrenrasse" einläuten sollte. Alle Publikationen und Vereine, die sich diesen Vorstellungen widersetzen oder sich nicht vereinnahmen lassen wollten, wurden kurzerhand verboten.

Ausgerechnet diese von der NSDAP annektierte und umdefinierte Bewegung, die deutsche Nacktkultur, diente nach dem Krieg vor allem der katholischen Kirche, die sich in West-Deutschland um Rückgewinnung ihrer Macht bemühte, als Beweis für die „moralische Perversion" der Nazis.

In den fünfziger Jahren bis in die Sechziger hinein, war es ein besonderes Anliegen der kirchlichen und kirchentreuen Sittenwächter, dass sämtliche Publikationen der Lebensreformer auch weiterhin verboten blieben. Versuche, einige

Magazine neu zu beleben, scheiterten oftmals an purer Gewalt. Kioske, die diese verkauften, gingen dabei in Flammen auf, Buchhändler wurden wegen der Verbreitung von Pornografie angezeigt, Druckereien verweigerten die Herstellung auch aus Angst vor Auftragsverlusten. Dass dieser Zensur nichts Wesentliches entgegen gesetzt wurde, hatte vor allem einen Grund: die Deutschen hatten mit dem Wiederaufbau und dem einfachen Überleben alle Hände voll zu tun. Auf diese Freiheit schien man verzichten zu können. Tatsächlich gewannen die christlich-konservativen und anti-sozialistischen Kräfte in der Bundesrepublik Deutschland derart an Boden, dass erst nach Einsetzen der linken Stundentenbewegung 1968 und der damit unter anderem einher gehenden sexuellen Liberalisierung der nackte Körper selbst nicht mehr als pornografisch gesehen wurde.

Erst danach konnte sich im Westen eine neue, wenn auch apolitische, Freikörperkultur entwickeln.

Anders dagegen verlief es für die deutschen Sonnenanbeter in der 1949 gegründeten DDR. Auch aus purer Opposition gegen den konservativen Westen und in Rückbesinnung auf die Arbeiterwurzeln der Naturalistenbewegung und deren Gleichheitsgedanke duldete die sozialistische Regierung, wenn auch stark kontrolliert und reglemetiert, das Nacktbaden an den meisten Seen und Badestränden. Noch heute, 20 Jahre nach der Wiedervereinigung befinden sich die meisten FKK-Strände und -Seen in der damaligen DDR. Es ist sogar in einigen Regionen eine Besonderheit, nicht die Strandabschnitte zu kennzeichnen, auf denen Nacktbaden erlaubt ist, sondern wo Besucher verpflichtet sind, Bekleidung zu tragen. Der „Textilstrand“ zeigt deutlich, dass der bekleidete deutsche Sonnenanbeter hier eher eine Minderheit darstellt.

Sexuality in the Third Reich

Axel Lawaczeck

Orgies on the Obersalzberg. Excesses in the SA and NSDAP offices. Porn productions for foreign currencies. Twilight bars serving the Gestapo. Diplomats and generals moaning state secrets into silk cushions between the thighs of loyal prostitutes, while the Germans say goodbye to lust under the whip of surveillance and repression. A true representation of sexuality in Germany from 1933 to 1945? Hardly. Sometimes, very dark times arouse very dark fantasies. However, truth is much more down to earth.

Bigotry and hypocrisy characterised the sexuality under the brown terror rule. Propaganda Minister Joseph Goebbels, who on the outside played the role of caring father of six and the loving husband of his wife Magda Goebbels, is a notorious womanizer. Street jargon called him the Babels-

berg buck. He said he was opposed to Philistines and had nothing against wholesome sensuality. As the top responsible head of the national-socialist media industry, he was also the boss of the UFA movie production halls of Potsdam-Babelsberg. Many of the secret jokes of the time illustrate that Goebbels, a very tiny man, with a lame foot, was not an Adonis. "Dear God, make me blind, to believe Goebbels is of Arian kind." Probably, his almost unlimited power was his ability to force many famous actresses into his bed. When he fell in love with celebrity Lída Baarová and wanted to leave his Arian prototype family, Hitler intervened personally and put an end to the affair.

Hitler saw the German woman mainly as the German mother. Her traditional role was systematically magnified under the national-socialist regime and exploited for propaganda. "The most wonderful duty that truly fulfils woman is to give children to her people." This doctrine was supported by financial subsidies and by the award of orders, to women with "outstanding birth rates." The Mother's Cross In Gold for instance, was awarded to mothers of eight and more children. All that was done under strange racist-biological concepts of the NS-ideology. The condition for the award was "that the parents of the children are of true Germanic blood and fit for heritage, the mother is worthy of the award, and the children are born healthy." The aim was to spread Arian ideology, and to replace the millions of soldiers who lost their lives for the Third Reich.

The Reichsführer SS Heinrich Himmler was not that close to the traditional role of family man. Towards Hitler, he even supported bigamy in favour of higher birth rates, and gave out an SS-internal order to procrastinate children

out of wedlock to fulfil the highest Arian standards. The unofficial order got stuck. The fear of offending the overwhelming sexual morality of the German population was too big. Many of the anti-human breeding concepts of Himmler, blossomed behind closed doors. Sexual liberty remained a privilege of the SS-elite, while ordinary people had to stick to law and order.

Sex in the Third Reich: this subject is bound to raise wild speculation. Probably because one would assume a regime that broke all taboos would not refrain from anything weird. However, it was rather an anti-lust period, when sexuality blossomed more in hidden privacy, unless one belonged to the powers that ruled. Homosexuality and prostitution were punished fiercely, up to concentration camp. The possession of pornographic books, pictures and films was strictly prohibited. Of course, this did not keep the lying representatives of the ruling regime from dealing with confiscated erotica on the international markets in order to cash foreign currencies. Double moral standards were the measure they used. Reinhard Heydrich, director of the Reichssicherheitshauptamt, in March 1935 gave permission to sell copies of the seized pornographic collection of writer Eduard Fuchs in Paris. The profit from the sales was 30.670 Francs.

Sexualität im Dritten Reich

Axel Lawaczeck

Orgien auf dem Obersalzberg. Exzesse in den Büros von SA und NSDAP. Pornoproduktionen zur Beschaffung von Devisen. Und schummrige Salons im Dienste der Gestapo, in denen Diplomaten und Generäle zwischen den Schenkeln linientreuer Kurtisanen Staatsgeheimnisse in die seidenen Kissen stöhnen, während das deutsche Volk unter der Knute von Überwachung und Repression der Lust entsagt. Sah so die deutsche Sexualität zwischen den Jahren 1933 und 1945 aus? Wohl kaum. Manchmal wecken besonders dunkle Zeiten eben besonders schmutzige Fantasien. Indes: die Wahrheit ist wesentlich profaner.

Bigotterie und Heuchlerei prägen die Sexualität in der Zeit des braunen Terrors: so ist zum Beispiel Propagandaminister Joseph Goebbels, der nach außen den treusorgenden Vater von sechs Kindern und den liebenden Ehemann seiner Frau Magda Goebbels gibt, ein berüchtigter Schür-

zenjäger. Im Volksmund nennt man ihn den Bock von Babelsberg. Und er selbst sagt, er sei gegen pfäffisches Muckertum und habe nichts gegen eine gesunde Sinnlichkeit. Als obersten Verantwortlichen der nationalsozialistischen Medienindustrie unterstehen ihm auch die UFA-Filmproduktionsstätten in Potsdam-Babelsberg. Viele Flüsterwitze aus dieser Zeit verdeutlichen, dass Goebbels, von kleinwüchsiger Gestalt und mit einen Klumpfuß ausgestattet, nicht gerade ein Adonis ist. „Lieber Gott, mach mich blind, dass ich Goebbels arisch find." Wohl nur aufgrund seiner nahezu uneingeschränkten Macht gelingt es ihm, viele Schauspielerinnen in sein Bett zu zwingen. Als er schließlich in Liebe zur gefeierten Lída Baarová entbrennt und sich von seiner arischen Musterfamilie trennen will, interveniert Hitler persönlich und beendet die Affäre.

Hitler selbst sieht in der deutschen Frau vor allem eine deutsche Mutter. Ihre traditionelle Rolle wird während des nationalsozialistischen Regimes systematisch verherrlicht und propagandistisch aufgewertet. „Die wunderbarste Aufgabe, die eine Frau erfüllen kann, ist die, ihrem Volk Kinder zu schenken" – diese Doktrin wird durch finanzielle Förderungsprogramme eifrig unterstützt, aber auch durch die Verleihung von Orden an Frauen mit „überdurchschnittlicher Gebärleistung". So gibt es das Mutterkreuz in Gold für Mütter mit acht und mehr Kindern. All dies geschieht unter den verqueren rassebiologischen Gesichtspunkten der NS-Ideologie: Voraussetzung für die Verleihung ist, „dass die Eltern der Kinder deutschblütig und erbtüchtig, die Mütter der Auszeichnung würdig und die Kinder lebend geboren sind". Es geht um die Verbreitung des Ariertums – und darum, die millionenfach gefallenen Soldaten des tausendjährigen Reiches zu ersetzen.

Wenig anfangen mit dem traditionellen Familienbild kann wiederum der Reichsführer SS Heinrich Himmler, der Hitler gegenüber zugunsten höherer Geburtenzahlen sogar die Bigamie befürwortet und einen SS-internen Befehl zur Zeugung unehelicher Kinder erlässt, die höchsten arischen Ansprüchen genügen sollen. Doch es bleibt bei dieser inoffiziellen Anordnung: die Angst, die vorherrschende Sexualmoral der deutschen Bevölkerung zu verletzen, ist zu groß. So blühen viele der menschenverachtenden Zuchtideen Himmlers im Verborgenen – und sexuelle Freizügigkeit bleibt ein Privileg der SS-Elite, während für das Volk Zucht und Ordnung gelten.

Sex im Dritten Reich: bei diesem Thema kommt es immer wieder zu wilden Spekulationen – vermutlich, weil man einem Regime, das vor keinem Tabu Halt gemacht hat, alles zutraut. Doch es war wohl vor allem eine lustfeindliche Zeit, in der man seine Sexualität lieber im Verborgenen auslebte, wenn man nicht zu den Machthabern gehörte.

Homosexualität und Prostitution wurden mit aller Härte bis hin zum Konzentrationslager bestraft, der Besitz pornografischer Bücher, Bilder und Filme war strengstens verboten. Was die verlogenen Vertreter des Regimes jedoch nicht daran hinderte, mit konfiszierten Erotika auf dem internationalen Markt Handel zu treiben, um an Devisen zu gelangen. Doppelte Moral war auch hier das Maß aller Dinge: Reinhard Heydrich, Chef des Reichssicherheitshauptamtes, genehmigte im März 1935 höchstpersönlich den Verkauf von Doubletten aus der beschlagnahmten pornografischen Sammlung des Schriftstellers Eduard Fuchs in Paris. Der Gewinn betrug 30.670 Francs.

Zum

Andenken

an

schöne

Stunden

Deine

Erika

Sexuality, Pornography, and Censoring

Dr. Elfsieben

Sex and death are the strongest stimuli, and the greatest secrets. "Das Mysterium Frau und das Mysterium des Bösen" (Horst Herrmann) is fascinating, whether as "Eros and Thanatos" in science and high culture or as "Sex and Violence" in the entertainment industry, especially because both are withdrawn from conscious control, pointing towards the naked truth.

The anarchic tendency of the ecstatic "being out of oneself" makes physical forms of art not only especially exciting for producers and consumers, but also especially dangerous in the eyes of the state and the guardians of morals and youth. They want to control body-focused genres such as pornography and horror, which excite instinctive feelings such as lust or fear, by bans and censoring. They claim otherwise human dignity would be affected or rot away. In fact however, the norms and values are more about the fear ruling powers have, of losing control.

This race between supporters and opponents of pornography is as old as the subject itself. As soon as a new medium was invented, erotica, sex, lust or pornography were represented in it, and the officials tried to suppress it. With the invention of photography in the 19th century, even those who were not talented as artists and came from uneducated classes, could produce all one could imagine, easily and cheaply and distribute it clandestinely.

The act §184 was introduced when the Reich was founded in 1871. It was liberalized only with the reform of the criminal code in 1973, yet in a modified form, it is valid until today. The paragraph prohibited "sodomy", which included the distribution of uncouth texts, illustrations or representations that grossly infringed against the modesty of normal people.

Whether Kaiserreich, Weimar Republic, „Third Reich", German Democratic Republic or Federal Republic of Germany: § 184 and many other acts on the protection of youth, for instance the "act on protecting youth against dirt and trash" of 1926, gave the ruling powers the instruments to use against slippery theatre plays such as Frank Wedekind's „Die Büchse der Pandora" or Arthur Schnitzler's „Der Reigen" and against "uncouth trash novels" by de Sade ("Justine") Zola ("Nana") or Balzac ("Drollige Erzählungen/Conte Droles"). Lascivious postcards, "obscene" serial novels or the first wobbly black-and-white films with naked skin, excited the vice police. Since 1920, film censoring was reasoned by virtue of the "Lichtspielgesetz Act on movies". Even reproductions of artwork, for instance paintings of Rubens, Rodin or Canova had to be taken out of shop windows. Still, the porn of the founders' days sold

under the table in masses. This is proven by collections such as the "Rotenberg Collection." Some of this old "Forbidden Erotica" is still on the index in the 21st century.

The climate of the young Federal Republic of Germany was not lust-friendly. Willi Forst's melodramatic movie "Die Sünderin" (1950) was prohibited because of a short scene with actress Hildegard Knef in the nude and the beautification of prostitution and suicide. In 1949 the voluntary self-control organisation of the movie industry "Freiwillige Selbstkontrolle der Filmwirtschaft," short FSK, was set-up. This institution ordered age restrictions and cuts to be made. The act on the distribution of youth-endangering publications "Gesetz über die Verbreitung jugendgefährdender Schriften" was adopted in 1954. The office, which was to enforce this law, was set-up in 1954 under the name "Bundesprüfstelle für jugendgefährdende Schriften". It started with indexing comic strips, gents' night chants such as "Der Novak lässt mich nicht verkommen," gay magazines and a lot of nude illustrations. The things that were indexed to protect the youth: Sacher-Masoch's "Venus im Pelz" (1958 ind.) de Sade's "Philosophie im Boudoir" (1963), Burroughs' "Naked Lunch" (1964) Clelands "Memoiren der Fanny Hill" (1964) and Apollinaire's "Elftausend Ruten" (1971) to name but a few classical works. In the days of chancellor Adenauer, even sexual education such as "Illustrierte Wörterbuch des Sexuallebens" by Dr. med. W. Feyerabend was indexed in1954 and volume 14/1959 of the satire magazine "Simplicissimus" was seized because of the "almost unveiled representation of a nipple." The novel "Josefine Mutzenbacher," anonymously published about 1900, was long available only as a private reprint under the counter. In 1968, a publisher

house edition was confiscated. The legal dispute went up to the Constitutional Court Bundesverfassungsgericht, which in the 1990s stated that pornography might be a form of art. Still, this book is indexed until today. After a nation-wide confiscation and indexing in the 1980s, Henry Miller's "Opus Pistorum" was recently let off the hook.

Cinemas also were difficult territory for sex to begin with. Ingmar Bergman's "Das Schweigen," for instance aroused a scandal with a masturbation scene. In 1964, this lead to the set-up of the "Aktion Saubere Leinwand." Educational movies, for instance by Oswalt Kolle, had a lot of trouble with the authorities from 1968-1972 with movies like "Dein Mann, das unbekannte Wesen." This trouble however did not reduce his success. Prohibition tends to rouse interest. Other bans on pornography that made history were for example Nagisa Oshima's "Im Reich der Sinne," Pasolini's "Saló oder die letzten 120 Tage von Sodom" and "Die Geschichte der O." By now, most of the bans have been revoked. "Hard-core pornography" however, is still subject to a total ban, while private possession is permitted. With child and youth pornography, private possession is also a crime.

Sexualität, Pornografie, Zensur

Dr. Elfsieben

Sex und Tod sind die stärksten Reize und größten Geheimnisse. „Das Mysterium Frau und das Mysterium des Bösen" (Horst Herrmann) fasziniert, ob als „Eros und Thanatos" in Wissenschaft und Hochkultur, oder als „Sex and Violence" in der Unterhaltungsindustrie gerade deswegen, weil sich beides der bewussten Steuerung entzieht und einen Blick auf die nackte Wahrheit gewährt.

Die anarchische Tendenz des ekstatischen „Außer-sich-Seins" macht körperbezogene Kunstformen nicht nur besonders aufregend für Produzenten und Konsumenten, sondern in den Augen von Staat, Sittenwächtern und Jugendschützern auch besonders gefährlich. Vor allem Körpergenres wie Pornografie und Horror, die instinktive Gefühle wie Lust oder Angst erregen, sollen durch Verbote und Zensur kontrolliert werden, da die Menschenwürde verletzt würde oder Verrohung drohe. Im Grunde geht es bei den Normen und Werten aber wohl eher um die Angst der Machthaber vor Kontrollverlust.

Dieser Wettlauf zwischen Pornografieverfechtern und -verfolgern ist so alt wie das Thema selbst. Sobald ein neues Medium erfunden war, wurden auch Erotik, Sexlust oder Pornografie dargestellt und von Behördenseite aus zu unterdrücken versucht. Mit Erfindung der Fotografie im 19. Jahrhundert konnten auch künstlerisch Unbegabte womöglich aus ungebildeten Schichten einfach und billig alles Mögliche herstellen und heimlich vertreiben.

Der schon bei der Reichsgründung 1871 eingeführte und erst mit der Strafrechtsreform 1973 liberalisierte, in abgewandelter Form aber bis heute gültige, Strafrechtsparagraph 184 verbot „Unzüchtigkeit", und somit die Verbreitung von unsittlichen Schriften, Abbildungen oder Darstellungen, die das Schamgefühl normaler Personen gröblich verletzten.

Ob Kaiserreich, Weimarer Republik, „Drittes Reich", DDR oder Bundesrepublik Deutschland: Mit dem Paragraf 184 und zahlreichen Jugendschutzgesetzen wie dem „Gesetz zur Bewahrung der Jugend vor Schmutz und Schund" von 1926 war es der Obrigkeit möglich, ebenso gegen schlüpfrige Theaterstücke wie Frank Wedekinds „Die Büchse der Pandora" oder Arthur Schnitzlers „Der Reigen" vorzugehen, wie gegen „Schmutz- und Schundliteratur" von de Sade („Justine"), Zola („Nana") oder Balzac („Drollige Erzählungen"). Auch laszive Postkarten, „obszöne" Kolportageromane oder die ersten verwackelten Schwarzweißstreifen mit entblößter Haut erregten die Sittenwächter, die seit 1920 ihre Filmzensur mit dem „Lichtspielgesetz" begründen konnten. Selbst Reproduktionen von Kunstwerken z.B. von Rubens, Rodin oder Canova mussten aus Schaufenstern entfernt werden. Gleichwohl verkaufte sich der „Gründerzeitschweinkram" massenhaft unter der Hand, wie einschlägige Sammlungen wie die „Rotenberg Collection" belegen. Diese alte „Forbidden Erotica" wird gelegentlich noch im 21. Jahrhundert indiziert.

Auch in der jungen Bundesrepublik herrschte ein eher lustfeindliches Klima, wie etwa das Verbot von Willi Forsts Melodrama „Die Sünderin“ 1950 wegen einer kurzen Nacktszene von Hildegard Knef und der angeblichen Verharmlosung von Prostitution und Suizid zeigt. Bereits 1949 war die „Freiwillige Selbstkontrolle der Filmwirtschaft“ FSK gegründet worden, die Altersfreigaben und Schnittauflagen verfügt. 1953 wurde das „Gesetz über die Verbreitung jugendgefährdender Schriften“ erlassen und 1954 die mit der Durchführung beauftragte „Bundesprüfstelle für jugendgefährdende Schriften“ gegründet. Sie indizierte zunächst vor allem Comics, Herrenabend-Chansons wie „Der Novak lässt mich nicht verkommen“, Schwulen-Zeitschriften und allerlei Nacktbildchen. Was nicht alles wegen Jugendgefährdung auf den Index kam: Sacher-Masochs „Venus im Pelz“ (1958 ind.), de Sades „Philosophie im Boudoir“ (1963), Burroughs „Naked Lunch“ (1964), Clelands „Memoiren der Fanny Hill“ (1964) und Apollinaires „Elftausend Ruten“ (1971), um nur einige Klassiker zu nennen. In der Adenauer-Ära wurden sogar Aufklärungsratgeber wie das „Illustrierte Wörterbuch des Sexuallebens“ von Dr. med. W. Feyerabend 1954 indiziert und Heft 14/1959 der Satirezeitschrift „Simplicissimus“ wegen der „fast unverhüllten Wiedergabe der Brustwarze“ beschlagnahmt. Der um 1900 anonym verfasste Roman „Josefine Mutzenbacher“ war lange nur als Privatdruck unter der Hand erhältlich. 1968 wurde eine Verlagsausgabe verboten. Der Rechtsstreit ging bis zum Bundesverfassungsgericht, das in den 1990er Jahren feststellte, dass auch Pornografie Kunst sein könne. Dennoch ist das Buch bis heute indiziert. Wieder vom Haken gelassen wurde hingegen nach bundesweiter Beschlagnahme und Indizierung in den 1980er Jahren Henry Millers „Opus Pistorum“.

Auch im Kino hatte es Sex zunächst schwer, sei es in Ingmar Bergmans „Das Schweigen", der wegen einer Selbstbefriedigungsszene zum Skandal wurde und 1964 zur Gründung der „Aktion Saubere Leinwand" führte, oder die Aufklärungsstreifen von Oswalt Kolle, der 1968-1972 mit Filmen wie „Dein Mann, das unbekannte Wesen" mehr als einmal Ärger mit den Kontrollbehörden bekam. Was den Erfolg aber nicht schmälerte, denn Verbote machen ja erst recht scharf. Andere Pornografieverbote, die in die Annalen eingingen, waren etwa Nagisa Oshimas „Im Reich der Sinne", Pasolinis „Saló oder die letzten 120 Tage von Sodom" und „Die Geschichte der O". Sie sind heute zwar zumeist aufgehoben, „harte Pornografie" (mit Gewalt oder Tieren) unterliegt aber weiterhin einem Totalverbot, wobei der private Besitz erlaubt ist. Nur bei Kinder- und Jugendpornografie ist auch das strafbar.

Amateur Erotica

Boris von Brauchitsch

The wife on the sofa, the couple under the coffee table – modern technology such as flash and automatic release, turned private homes into playgrounds of sexual extravaganza, since the 20s, and even more so since the 40s. The quality of photos however, strongly differs from professional studio photography of the same time or earlier. Private photos often have the charm of snapshots. They are absolutely unspoilt by good advice from photographic textbooks. Wobbling lines, heads cut off and poor contrasts are the perfect successors, to the working-class settings of fitted cupboards, oil paintings and bric-a-brac, where the urge is distilled into prohibited photos. A large number of the photos in this volume come from this private world. This chapter shows but a few crude examples that illustrate how the need to make the personal, erotic and one's own sexual life, immortal.

Pornography had been an upper class luxury for centuries. Until late in the 19th century, it was concealed in secret museums away from the lower classes and from women. Only when the number of illiterates in society dropped, did the need rise, to control the obscene in literature more strongly. Art becoming more democratic and bourgeois obviously seemed to make state control of decency inevitable. The lower classes conquering pornography as soon as they had the required means seemed a natural development, almost an act of emancipation.

After the introduction of women's suffrage in Germany, in 1918 (and two years later in the USA), and the expansion on the magazine market of the Weimar Republic – 400 different magazines were published in Berlin alone – women were discovered as a target group for advertising to be reckoned with. The mirror, originally a symbol of vanity and mortality, turned up in advertising; woman watching, reflecting and rating herself. Not only goods for perfect housekeeping but also fashion and cosmetics aimed at woman as the responsible, as well as pretty housekeeper and extravagant and well groomed representative of a successful man were presented. The conscious use of female attraction was openly advertised as a necessity, when looking for a husband and a condition for the success of partnerships. The wife was turned into a sex object, out in the open.

This trend was also manifested in domestic photo production. The fleeting image of the mirror was replaced by the everlasting self-mirroring with the camera. The only inhibition hindering the sexual act to turn into domestic pornography was the photo laboratory, which was hard to do without. Not all amateurs had darkrooms of their own. Many were forced to go on an embarrassing tour of photo shops to develop and magnify their films. Only when video and digital cameras conquered the market, did this last rather week public control institution fall and private porn production become inflationary.

Amateur-Erotika

Boris von Brauchitsch

Die Gattin auf dem Sofa, das Paar unterm Couchtisch – dank moderner Technik, wie Blitz und Selbstauslöser, wurden die eigenen vier Wände seit den 20er Jahren und vermehrt seit den 40ern zur Spielwiese sexueller Eskapaden. Was öffentlich verpönt war, wurde im Privaten zelebriert. Die Qualität der Fotos unterscheidet sich allerdings deutlich von den professionellen Studio-Aufnahmen, die zur gleichen Zeit und früher entstanden, hat eher den Charme von Schnappschüssen und bleibt von guten Ratschlägen aus Fotolehrbüchern absolut unberührt. Stürzende Linien, abgeschnittene Köpfe und flaue Kontraste sind die lupenreine Fortführung der kleinbürgerlichen Szenerie aus Schrankwänden, Ölschinken und Nippes-Boards in der der Trieb in verbotene Bilder verwandelt wird. Ein Großteil der Aufnahmen dieses Bandes stammt aus jenem privaten Kosmos. In diesem Kapitel sind nur einige markante Beispiele versammelt, die das Bedürfnis nach Verewigung der persönlichen Erotik und des eigenen Sexualverkehrs besonders eindringlich veranschaulichen.

Pornografie war zunächst einmal über Jahrhunderte ein Luxus der Oberschicht und wurde bis ins 19. Jahrhundert hinein in geheimen Museen vor den unteren Klassen und den Frauen verborgen. Erst mit einem deutlichen Schwund an Analphabeten in der Gesellschaft war es geboten, das Obszöne auch in der Literatur stärker zu kontrollieren. Die Demokratisierung und Verbürgerlichung der Künste machte im Gegenzug eine staatliche Regulierung des Anständigen offenbar unumgänglich. Dass sich auch die unteren Schichten der Pornografie bemächtigten, sobald ihnen die dafür notwendigen Möglichkeiten zur Verfügung standen, scheint eine selbstverständliche Entwicklung, geradezu ein Akt der Emanzipation zu sein.

Nach Einführung des Frauenwahlrechts in Deutschland im Jahr 1918 (in den USA zwei Jahre später) und der Expansion auf dem Zeitschriftenmarkt der Weimarer Republik – allein in Berlin gab es rund 400 verschiedene Magazine – wurden Frauen als ernstzunehmende Zielgruppe der Werbung ausgemacht. Der Spiegel, ursprünglich Symbol für Eitelkeit und Vergänglichkeit, tauchte dort zunehmend auf: die Frau betrachtet, reflektiert und beurteilt sich selbst. Nicht nur die Waren für einen perfekten Haushalt, sondern vor allem auch Mode und Kosmetik zielten auf die Frau als verantwortungsbewusste und wohlgefällige Hüterin des Heims und extravagante und gepflegte Repräsentantin eines erfolgreichen Mannes. Der bewusste Einsatz weiblicher Reize wurde offen als Notwendigkeit bei der Gattensuche und dann als Teil partnerschaftlichen Erfolgs propagiert. Unverhohlen wurde die Ehefrau zum Sexobjekt.

Dieser Trend schlug sich auch in der heimischen Fotoproduktion nieder. Das flüchtige Bild des Spiegels wurde ersetzt durch die überdauernde Selbstbespiegelung mit Hilfe der Kamera. Die einzige Hemmschwelle bei der heimischen Verwandlung des Sexualakts in Pornografie war das Fotolabor, das sich oft nur schwer umgehen ließ. Nicht jeder Amateur hatte eine eigene Dunkelkammer, und so war mancher gezwungen, die Peinlichkeit auf sich zu nehmen und die Filme zur Entwicklung und Vergrößerung in den Fotoladen zu tragen. Erst mit Video und Digitalkamera fiel diese letzte und ohnehin eher schwache Instanz öffentlicher Kontrolle und machte die private Porno-Produktion endgültig inflationär.

Sex and Socialism

Hans Bosch

Officially, pornography was non-existent in the former socialist GDR (Eastern Germany). No more than a few photos of nude models, found here and there in fashion or satire magazines, was all there was to be had. They corresponded to not very wild, amateurish and bourgeois nude photography. Frequently, the illustrations showed nude naturalists (FKK) rather than strongly sexually stimulating pornography. Unofficially however, there were amateur film clubs, where people with the same intention met to produce porn movies. In the GDR, it was hardly possible for private persons to buy equipment or material for filming (e.g. 16mm Orwo Film). This means these porn-producing groups were mainly formed out of existing creative groups in the people's own factories. Their actual task was the production of films focusing on the achievements and success of socialism. These films were produced clandestinely and shown only to select porn lovers or other befriended amateur groups. There are allegations that the GDR had a state-operated, secret porn production business, to sell the products abroad, for profits in foreign currencies. However, to date, there is no evidence for this allegation.

Sex und Sozialismus

Hans Bosch

In der ehemaligen sozialistischen DDR gab es offiziell keine Pornografie. Was zu bekommen war, ging über ein paar Fotos von Nackten, die man vereinzelt in Mode- oder Satiremagazinen fand, nicht hinaus. Sie entsprachen einer nicht sehr wilden, amateurhaft bürgerlichen Aktfotografie. Oft waren es Abbildungen mit FKKlerinnen (Frei Körper Kultur), jedoch keinesfalls stark sexuell stimulierende Pornografie. Inoffiziell formierten sich allerdings in Amateurfilmzirkeln Gleichgesinnte zur Erstellung von Pornofilmen. Da es in der DDR für Privatpersonen kaum möglich war, an Equipment bzw. Filmmaterial (z. B. der 16 mm Orwo Film) heranzukommen, entstanden diese Porno-„Produktions“-Zirkel meist aus vorhandenen kreativen Zirkeln der volkseigenen Betriebe. Deren eigentliche Aufgabe war die Erstellung von Filmen, die die Leistungen und Errungenschaften des Sozialismus in den Fokus stellten. Diese „getarnt“ produzierten Filme wurden dann auch nur ausgewählten Pornoliebhabern oder anderen befreundeten Amateur-Zirkeln gezeigt. Es wird zwar behauptet, die DDR hätte eine geheime staatliche Pornoproduktion betrieben um deren Produkte Gewinn und Devisen bringend ins Ausland zu verkaufen, diese Vermutung hat sich aber bis heute nicht bekräftigt.

Sexual Revolution

Hans Bosch

The term "sexual revolution" was used for the first time in 1936 in the work "Die Sexualität im Kulturkampf" published by Wilhelm Reich. In this work, Reich criticized the hypocritic sexual morality of his time. He was convinced that the double moral standards in force, in society in these days, suppressed the sexual drive. Consequently, this restricted creativity and fostered frustration and aggression, which again promoted a hierarchical principle of power. Reich and other authors in the sixties, claimed that the fear of the younger generation, of fixed structures and repetitive authoritative systems was very big, caused by the experience with the Nazi regime.

In the early sixties, couples married very young. This was the most common way to live out erotic desires without repressions. One third of all brides was already pregnant or with child on her wedding day. Every year, there were more than a million prohibited abortions, of which 15,000 on average, were lethal. This was caused by repressive legislation and lack of sexual education. The so-called "Heavenly Police Rules" banned all advertising for contraception into the sixties. Until the end of the sixties, the so-called "law on coupling" was still in force, which prohibited relatives, friends or landlords to provide accommodation for unmarried couples. Then, it was virtually impossible to live together without being married. The youth movement of 1968 shook of the oppression of the "Philistine hypocrites" and discovered sexual experimentation. Alternative lifestyles and co-habitation developed, with free sexual encounters. However, the launch of the contraceptive pill caused the greatest change for the majority of society. This wide social opening also led to the liberalisation of laws on sexuality. Sexuality was used more and more frequently for commercial purposes in magazines, film and TV: the so-called sex wave.

Sexuelle Revolution

Hans Bosch

Der Begriff sexuelle Revolution taucht zum ersten Mal 1936 in dem von Wilhelm Reich veröffentlichten Werk „Die Sexualität im Kulturkampf“ auf. Darin kritisierte Reich die verlogene Sexualmoral seiner Zeit. Die in seinen Augen herrschende Doppelmoral der damaligen Gesellschaft führe zur Unterdrückung des sexuellen Triebs. In der Konsequenz führe dies zu einer Einschränkung der Kreativität, zu Frustration und Aggression. Dies fördere wiederum ein hierarchisches Herrschaftsprinzip. Reich und andere Schriftsteller postulierten in den Sechzigern, dass durch die Erfahrungen mit dem Naziregime die Furcht der jüngeren Generation vor festen Strukturen und wiederkehrenden autoritären Systemen sehr groß war.

Zu Beginn der Sechziger heirateten Paare recht früh. Dies war der gängigste Weg, ihre Erotik ohne Repressionen ausleben zu können. Ein Drittel der Bräute war am Tag der Eheschließung bereits schwanger oder hatte ein Kind.

Pro Jahr fanden über eine Million verbotener Schwangerschafts-Abbrüche statt, davon endeten im Durchschnitt 15.000 tödlich. Ursache war die repressive Gesetzgebung und eine völlig fehlende sexuelle Aufklärung. Die so genannte „Himmlische Polizeiverordnung“ verbot bis in die sechziger Jahre jegliche Werbung für Verhütungsmittel. Bis Ende der Sechziger gab es z.B. den „Kuppeleiparagraphen“, welcher Familienangehörigen, Bekannten und Vermietern verbot, unverheirateten Paaren Räumlichkeiten zur Verfügung zu stellen. Damals war es fast unmöglich unverheiratet zusammen zu leben. Die 68er Jugendbewegung befreite sich von den Zwängen des „Spießertums“, wurde sexuell experimentierfreudiger. Es entstanden alternative Lebensformen des Zusammenlebens, die eine freizügiges sexuelles Miteinander pflegten. Die entscheidende Veränderung in der Mehrheit der Gesellschaft brachte aber die Einführung der Anti-Baby-Pille. Diese breite gesellschaftliche Öffnung führte auch zu einer Liberalisierung der die Sexualität betreffenden Gesetze. Es folgte eine wachsende kommerzielle Nutzung der Sexualität in Zeitschriften, Film und Fernsehen, die so genannte Sexwelle.

Source text - Quellenverzeichnis

Bleuel, H.P.: Sexual Society in Nazi Germany. Philadelphia. Lippincott, 1973

Franz X. Eder: Kultur der Begierde. Eine Geschichte der Sexualität. Beck, 2002

Michael Farin: Phantom Schmerz. Quellentexte zur Begriffsgeschichte des Masochismus, Belleville, April 2003

Shulamith Firestone: Frauenbefreiung und sexuelle Revolution, 1970

Peter Fuchs: Das Antlitz der Afrikanerin, Stuttgart, 1966

Gaspar, Ziehlke, Rothweiler (Herausgeber): Sittengeschichte des Zweiten Weltkrieges, Komet, 1980

Mel Gordon: Voluptuous Panic: The Erotic World of Weimar Berlin, Feral House, September 2008

Michael Grisko (Herausgeber): Freikörperkultur und Lebenswelt, Kassel university press, 1999

Birgit Haustedt: Die wilden Jahre in Berlin: Eine Klatsch- und Kulturgeschichte der Frauen, Edition Ebersbach, 1999

Dagmar Herzog: Die Politisierung der Lust. Sexualität in der deutschen Geschichte des 20. Jahrhunderts. Siedler, 2005

Heger, H.: The Men with the Pink Triangle. Boston: Alyson, 1980.

Manfred Herzer: Magnus Hirschfeld, Leben und Werk eines jüdischen, schwulen und sozialistischen Sexologen, Bibliothek rosa Winkel, 2001

Magnus Hirschfeld: Weltreise eines Sexualforschers. Eichborn, 2006

Lynn Hunt: Die Erfindung der Pornografie. Obszönität und die Erfindung der Moderne. Fischer, 1994

Michael Köhler (Herausgeber), Gisela Barche (Herausgeber): Das Aktfoto. Ästhetik, Geschichte, Ideologie. Ansichten vom Körper im fotografischen Zeitalter, Verlag Bucher, 1991

Stephanie Kuhnen: Butch Femme. Eine erotische Kultur, Querverlag, 1997

Thomas Kupfermann: Sommer, Sonne, Nackedeis. FKK in der DDR, Eulenspiegel, 2008

Niklaus Largier: Lob der Peitsch. Eine Kulturgeschichte der Erregung. Beck, 2001

Lautman, R.: The Pink Triangle, Journal of Homosexuality, Vol. 6 (1980), pp. 141-60.

Rainer Metzger: Berlin. Die 20er Jahre. Kunst und Kultur 1918-1933

Annette Miersch: Schulmädchen-Report: der deutsche Sexfilm der 70er Jahre. Berlin, Bertz + Fischer Verlag, 2003

Mosse, G.L.: Nazi Culture, New York, Grosset & Dunlap, 1966.

Plant, R.: The Pink Triangle: The Nazi War Against Homosexuals, New York: Holt, Rinehart & Winston, 1986

Wilhelm Reich: Die sexuelle Revolution, 1936, Neuaufl. 1966

Wilhelm Reich: Der Einbruch der sexuellen Zwangsmoral (1932; erw. u. revid. Aufl. 1972)

Wilhelm Reich: Der sexuelle Kampf der Jugend, 1932

Wilhelm Reich: Die Funktion des Orgasmus (psychoanalyt. Fachbuch 1927; erw. u. revid. u.d.T. Genitalität 1982)

Wilhelm Reich: Die Funktion des Orgasmus (u. gl. Titel wiss. Autobiographie 1942 engl.: 1969)

Reimut Reiche: Sexualität und Klassenkampf (Zur Kritik repressiver Entsublimierung), Berlin 1968

Heike Schader: Virile, Vamps und wilde Veilchen. Sexualität, Begehren und Erotik in den Zeitschriften homosexueller Frauen im Berlin der 1920er Jahre, Ulrike Helmer Verlag, 2004

Manfred Scheuch: Nackt. Kulturgeschichte eines Tabus im 20. Jahrh., Brandstätter, 2004

Claudia Schoppmann: Verbotene Verhältnisse. Frauenliebe 1938-1945, Querverlag, 1999

Roland Seim: Zwischen Medienfreiheit und Zensureingriffen, Telos Verlag 1997

Roland Seim: Der kommentierte Bildband ab "18". Zensur in der deutschen Kulturgeschichte, Telos Verlag 2001

Anna Maria Sigmund: Das Geschlechtsleben bestimmen wir: Sexualität im Dritten Reich, Verlag Heyne, 2008

Skrein, Christian: Secret Snapshots, Brandstätter Verlag, 2005

Gay Talese: Du sollst begehren – Auf den Spuren der sexuellen Revolution, Rogner und Bernhard Verlag, Berlin, 2007

Karl Heinrich Ulrichs zum 175. Geburtstag. Die Geschichte der Homosexualitäten und die schwule Identität an der Jahrtausendwende, Bibliothek rosa Winkel, 2000

Peter Weibel: Phantom der Lust. Visionen des Masochismus. Essays und Texte: 2, Belleville, April 2003

H.B.Wilson-DMK CO Bildarchiv: Copyright Abbildungen p. 67, 71, 82, 88, 90/91,167, 272

Arnd W.: thanks for the intruduction

Sexy Super Girls - Mike James
128 color pages/ISBN 978-3-936709-42-1
Special 3D Lenticular Hardcover/language: (GB) (D) (F) (E) (I)
"Sexy Super Girls" is a dynamite combination of fresh young girls with perfectly pimped-up bodies. These photos are playful and erotic, spicy and sweet, it's the stuff fantasies are made of. Prepare to be blown away!

Glamshots - hot & naked - Tom Veller
368 color pages/ISBN 978-3-936709-43-8
Hardcover/language: (GB) (D) (F) (E) (I)
"Glamshots: hot & naked" captures glamorous girls at their naughtiest, revealing everything for your pleasure. If you like girls who are young and up for anything, you won't want to put this book down!

Nylon Girls - Erotic Fashion Photography - Christine Kessler
112 color pages/ISBN 978-3-936709-38-4
padded hardcover/language: (GB) (D) (F) (E) (I)
Nylon Girls are revealed to you through the camera of Christine Kessler. She takes you on an erotic journey in the company of a harem of stunning beauties. Nylon Girls exposes the intimate secrets of these most sensual starlets. Erotic and daring, with a pinch of fetishism, for extra spice. A dish to be savoured over and over.

Erotic Dream Girls - Holly Randall
368 color pages/ISBN 978-3-936709-39-1/Hardcover/language: (GB) (D) (F) (E) (I)
Erotic Dream Girls is what it says and so much more. Holly Randall's provocative photography exposes some of the most beautiful girls on the planet. You have the privilege to see them just as she envisioned them, revealed, uninhibited and dazzling. The images captured by Randell's lens are sensual, intimate, exquisite, aesthetic and above all – sexy.

All Natural Girls - Martin Krake
368 color pages/ISBN 978-3-936709-40-7
Hardcover/language: (GB) (D) (F) (E) (I)
Beautiful. Natural. Young. Nude. There is no better way to describe Martin Krake's „All Natural Girls". Photographed in picturesque natural settings, the untamed and wild magnetism of these beauties easily outshines the locations. These girls are innocent, beautiful and will keep you salivating for more.

Kinky Nature - Emma Delves-Broughton - 112 color pages
padded hardcover (GB) (D) (F) (E) (I) ISBN 978-3-936709-41-4
Kinky Nature draws you into a dream forest, teeming with the kinkiest beauties in the land. Explore the wild side of these enchanting girls, whether they're lost in latex or wandering the forest naughtily nude. Fetish and frivolity come together leaving everything and nothing to the imagination. The sultry style of Emma Delves-Broughton's satiates your desire for wild abandonment and kinky natures.

Asia Bondage - Steven Speliotis
160 b&w pages/ ISBN 978-3-9807602-6-3
Hardcover/ language: (GB) (D) (F) (E) (I)
Asia Bondage, a highly erotic, exciting and thrilling journey through the light and shade of traditional black and white photography. An arousing shadow show of the senses.

Pornscapes - Pierre Radisic
128 b&w pages/ ISBN 978-3-936709-24-7
hardcover/ language: GB D F E I
Fascinatingly ambiguous though it is, Radisic's work remains eminently photographic. (...) The connection with reality, a crucial subject in photography is perverted in a controlled way, while the actual stucture of the picture is never altered. (...)

Bubble Bath Girls - Andrew Einhorn
368 color pages/ ISBN 978-3-936709-15-5
hardcover/ language: GB D F E I
Lather up and jump in!! Bubble Bath Girls drops you straight into a tub full of: naked, happy, soapy, sudsy New York Girls.

Art /Photography - Paul M. Smith
112 color pages/ ISBN 978-3-936709-10-0
hardcover/ language: GB D F E I
The sincerity and authority of the documentary is manipulated and questioned by Paul M Smith. Acting out Cindy Sherman for boys, he looks at the traditions of war and photography and the recreational aspects of life.

Bad Girls Hotel - Bob Coulter
368 color pages/ ISBN 978-3-936709-18-6
hardcover/ language: GB D F E I
Bob Coulter is back, down on his hands and knees shooting more of his Crazy Babes, this time at New York City's wildly unique Carlton Arms Hotel. Check out his colorful and explicit, humorous and bizarre photos in his long anticipated second book.

Guzzi Girls - Moe Moore - ISBN 978-3-936709-30-8
160 color pages/ hardcover/ language: GB D F E I
Guzzi Girls are a dream come true. Moe Moore's two favorite obsessions – vintage Moto Guzzis and beautiful girls – melt into each other perfectly ashe picks up the camera and shoots in his garage the hottest women around. The soft curves and bumps of the bike blend right into soft curves and bumpsof these women. Born to be wild, sexy and fun!

Naked Girls Smoking Weed - Robert Griffin
160 color pages/ ISBN 978-3-936709-26-1
hardcover/ language: GB D F E I
... features photos of naked girls smoking Marijuana from bongs, joints, blunts, pipes, hookahs, vaporizers, posing with plants, covered in buds and more. Each page includes an important fact about Hemp and/or Marijuana.

Stripped Naked - Peter Gorman
160 color pages/ ISBN 978-3-936709-13-1
hardcover/ language: GB D F E I
Models Stripped Naked of their inhibitions, exposing themselves once again for Gorman's camera. Raw, real and sexually charged. Powerful photographs of beautiful women.

Super Beauties - Dwayne Bell ISBN 978-3-936709-33-9
368 color pages/hardcover/language: GB D F E I
"Super Beauties is the most exquisite best-of selection from Body in Mind' unique nude art photo collection. 25 amateur photographers take the reader on a visual tour of more than 400 photos showcasing the world's most beautiful, freshest young women. The ultimate must-have for every aficionado of natural nude female beauty!"

Layley - John Donegan & Layley
160 b&w pages/ ISBN 978-3-938029-03-9
hardcover/ language: GB D F E I
Actually, John Donegan just wanted to photograph young Layley and her horse for an equestrian magazine. Then they left out the horse. Then her clothes. And finally all restrictions.

Champion - Walter Kundzicz
368 color pages/ISBN 978-3-936709-05-6
hardcover/ language: GB D F E I
During the late 1950s and early 60s, in the world of male physique photography the name Champion became synonymous with images of handsome, athletic young men captured in vivid color. Walter Kundzicz, the photographer who was Champion Studios created a diverse and fantasy-rich body of work.

Berlin Gay Mates - Karim Konrad
368 color pages/ ISBN 978-3-936709-23-0
hardcover/ language: GB D F E I
Karim Konrad's visual assault on the senses is overwhelming, and his models are ripe with their luscious youth. The artist's orgy of color explodes with sexiness and energy, pushing the viewer ever closer to a mental climax as he turns each page of this wonderful collection by this gifted newcomer.

TOUCH - Naked girls home alone - Peter Gorman
224 color pages/150 photos/ ISBN 978-3-936709-29-2
hardcover/ language: GB D F E I
Peter Gorman has been invited to join young, sexy women and watch them while they are home alone. The photos he took of these meetings are so intense, they make you feel like you were there. Join in and share these hot, yet intimate, private yet seductive moments.

Hot Luxury Girls - Tammy Sanborn
320 color pages/ ISBN 976-3-936709-34-6
hardcover/ language: GB D F E I
Elegant, stylish, enticing and ubersexy are the women on Tammy Sanborn's Hot Luxury Girls. Only the hottest models share their raw sexual and exquisite beauty in luxurious and sensual settings, dressed in the finest lingerie or classy nothingness. This high-end photo collection is truly a new definition of erotic chic!

My Favorite Model - 43 Photographers, 350 photos
320 color pages/ ISBN 978-3-936709-31-5
hardcover/ language: GB D F E I
It's all about the models. Without these extraordinary women erotic photography would not exist. 43 outstanding photographers from all over the world share their favorite model with us. 44 stunning beauties are put in the limelight and are paid homage to by the best in contemporary erotic photography. Let them take your breath away! Adore! Enjoy!

Pulp Fetish - Fred Berger
176 color pages/ ISBN 978-3-936709-27-8
hardcover/ language: (GB) (D) (F) (E) (I)
Inspired by the pulp comic books of his youth, legendary photographer & provocateur Fred Berger has compiled a body of work which fetishizes this vintage all-American genre to the point of orgasmic overload. Tales of the Wild West, of close-quarter combat, of cops and gangsters, pirates, super heroines and super villains – this is the stuff of PULP FETISH.

Desperado - Fred Berger
144 color pages/ ISBN 978-3-936709-25-4
padded hardcover/ language: (GB) (D) (F) (E) (I)
DESPERADO features the queer-fetish photography of Fred H. Berger, the man behind the "Propaganda", New York's legendary subculture zine. Famous for its drop-dead gorgeous androgyns wrapped in scandalous leather outfits and military uniforms, his body-of-work spans three decades and three continents.

BADLANDS - Charles Gatewood
448 b&w pages/ ISBN 978-3-9805876-4-8
language: (GB) (D) (F) (E) (I)
Gatewood's world is **freakish, earthy, blunt, erotic** – most of all **terribly and beautifully alive**.

Messy Girls! - Charles Gatewood
368 color pages/ ISBN 978-3-936709-00-1
hardcover/ language: (GB) (D) (F) (E) (I)
The new book of famous Photographer Charles Gatewood, showing over 340 **"Sploshing"** photographs of beautiful young fetish girls, naked and proud, smearing their nubile young bodies with pudding, honey and whipped cream, plus every messy substance imaginable.

Sexcats - Christopher Mealie
368 b&w pages/ ISBN 978-3-936709-06-3
hardcover/ language: (GB) (D) (F) (E) (I)
A collection of tawdry, yet titillating pictures from a sinful past. One would be hard pressed to find a greater collection of curvaceous kittens. Seductive, dark and always fun, over 350 fantastic images abound in this book of rare, vintage pinup and girly photos from the 1950s and 1960s. **Purrrfect.**"

UFO - Richard Brunswick
320 pages/ ISBN 978-3-9805876-3-1
color and b&w/ language: (GB) (D) (F) (E) (I)
Just landed! The ultimate picture bible for every UFO fan, the **most sensational and encompassing photo documentary** of the UFO century. Over **300 "never before publicized" pictures** of UFOs, scenes, contacts, evidence.... **Fantastic !!!**

Beluga - Jean V. Cleemput
174 color pages/ ISBN 978-3-936709-11-7
hardcover/ language: (GB) (D) (F) (E) (I)
Beluga, a ravissant mixture of exquisite snapshots of gorgeous nude models with tastebud-dazzling recipes. "Bon appetit!" High pro photography and absolute crazy!